Walk the Talk with Step 12

Walk the Talk with Step 12

Staying Sober through Service

GARY K.

Hazelden Publishing

Hazelden Publishing
Center City, Minnesota 55012
hazelden.org/bookstore

ISBN: 978-1-61649-659-3

Library of Congress Cataloging-in-Publication Data
is on file with the Library of Congress.

Editor's notes

The names, details, and circumstances may have been changed to protect the privacy of those mentioned in this publication.

This publication is not intended as a substitute for the advice of health care professionals.

Readers should be aware that websites listed in this work may have changed or disappeared between when this work was written and when it is read.

The Twelve Steps and Twelve Traditions are reprinted with permission of Alcoholics Anonymous World Services, Inc. ("A.A.W.S.") Permission to reprint the Twelve Steps and Twelve Traditions does not mean that A.A.W.S. has reviewed or approved the contents of this publication, or that A.A. necessarily agrees with the views expressed herein. A.A. is a program of recovery from alcoholism only—use of the Twelve Steps and Twelve Traditions in connection with programs and activities which are patterned after A.A., but which address other problems, or in any other non-A.A., does not imply otherwise.

Alcoholics Anonymous, AA, and the Big Book are registered trademarks of Alcoholics Anonymous World Services, Inc. The *Grapevine, AA Grapevine,* and *GV* are registered trademarks of The AA Grapevine, Inc.

20 19 18 17 16   1 2 3 4 5 6

Cover design: Theresa Jaeger Gedig
Interior design and typesetting: Percolator Graphic Design
Developmental editor: Sid Farrar
Production editor: Heather Silsbee

"The world seems to me excruciatingly, almost painfully beautiful at times, and the goodness and kindness of people often exceed that which even I expect."

—Lois Wilson

• • •

This book is dedicated in memory of my parents, Bruce and Mary Evelyn. Their unwavering unconditional love kept me alive against all odds through the darkest days of my active addiction.

Contents

❦

Introduction

*Having had a spiritual awakening as the result of these steps,
we tried to carry this message to alcoholics, and to practice
these principles in all our affairs.*

Step Twelve, Alcoholics Anonymous

No words can adequately express the gratitude I feel in my heart for the gifts I have personally received as a result of living in Step Twelve, which compels me to practice the principles of love, tolerance, and service in all of my affairs. Thanks to living in Step Twelve and being of service to the various fellowships to which I belong, it has not been necessary for me to take a drink or a drug since August 25, 1998. The Twelve Step program has given me an extraordinary life, and for that I am forever grateful.

As my personal mission is to carry the message of hope and the miracle of recovery to as many people as possible, making the commitment to write this book to sound a clarion call to action and light a Step Twelve grass fire is long overdue. There is a plague on planet Earth. Alcoholism and addiction to other drugs have reached pandemic proportions globally and have become one of America's most urgent public health issues. At this very moment, millions are sick and suffering alone in silence without knowledge of "the rooms" and the transformative healing power of Twelve Step recovery.

The battle against the epidemic of addiction and alcoholism is ongoing. New tools are needed to inspire those in recovery to heed the Twelfth Step call, and it is my goal for this book to give Twelve Steppers a time-tested way to take the hands of as many alcoholics and addicts as possible and help them along the path to the spiritual awakening and life of service—culminating in Step Twelve—that ensures long-term recovery.

A friend once told me a story about his grand sponsor (his sponsor's sponsor) who had been a guest at one of Bill W.'s dinner parties in New York. In order to engage Bill in conversation, he asked Bill, "What's the most important part of the program?," and without a second's hesitation, Bill replied, "Carry the message—Step Twelve." Bill went on to quip, "Never be so anonymous that it prevents you from helping someone. I know a fellow in Brooklyn who is so anonymous, I'm the only one who knows he's in the program."

One way or another, every alcoholic and addict will indeed "carry the message"—either by working Steps One through Eleven and then living in Step Twelve, or by becoming a statistic with a toe tag. At this moment in history—after eighty years of expansion of Twelve Step programs into well over one hundred nations—the toe tags still vastly outnumber the Twelve Steppers. Many of us believe this is due to the decline of service and the Twelfth Step call.

Each day thousands of addicts and alcoholics who are potential new members of our Twelve Step societies are released from detox and treatment facilities with little or no understanding about the vital nature of surrounding themselves with the loving wall of humanity found in the fellowship and of incorporating Step Twelve service into their lives in order to maintain long-term sobriety posttreatment. This condemns far too many of them to the revolving door of drunk tanks and rehabs—and for the vast majority, a trip to the morgue.

Privacy laws prevent us from marching into hospitals to work with drunks and addicts in the manner of Bill W., Dr. Bob, and the other founders in the early days of Alcoholics Anonymous (AA). As a result of their aggressive Twelve Stepping, our program flourished as it reached its peak in membership and efficacy over the decades that followed the publication of the Big Book in 1939, continuing until well into the 1960s. Today the efficacy of our program is in remission. The walk from the hospital, the jail, and rehabs to the rooms of recovery is a journey of a million miles without the fellowship of the spirit reaching out its hand to guide our sick friends on their road to recovery.

As you'll read in my story, during my third trip to rehab, a group of men from AA regularly brought meetings into the treatment center where I was in a thirty-day lockdown program. The day I came out of treatment, one of those men had travelled two hours by train so that he could be at the door of the treatment facility to greet me and shepherd me into "the rooms" and the fellowship. His name was Edgar W., a man with nearly forty years of sobriety whom I considered a saint. His father had been a member of Bill W.'s first AA group on Clinton Street in Brooklyn Heights. Edgar W., who became one of my sponsors, instilled in me the concept that once I have completed the first eleven Steps, my purpose, duty, and full-time job is to Twelfth Step everyone I meet.

It was also Bill W.'s emphatic admonition that our primary purpose is to be of maximum service to God and everyone around us, and to practice daily "the art of the Twelfth Step call."

The Fifth Tradition tells us that the primary purpose of every Twelve Step fellowship is to carry the message to those who still suffer; yet in today's busy, complicated world, too many in the fellowships seem to have retreated from that position as they chant "attraction not promotion." All too often, we sit in our church basements and say "let them come and find us." As a result, the epidemic tide of addiction rises as membership in Twelve Step fellowships decreases.

This book explores, redefines, and reinvigorates a passion for Step Twelve and the art of the Twelfth Step call. My hope and prayer is that it can embolden the faithful old guard while inspiring sponsors and their sponsees, new members, patients in treatment, and addiction professionals—a new generation of Twelve Step soldiers—to suit up with zeal, walk the talk, and carry the message to all of those who are still sick and suffering.

Since the heart of the Twelfth Step call is telling your story, I begin the book with my story, which makes up the three chapters of part 1, following the traditional formula—what it was like, what happened, and what it is like now. It's not only a tale of drinking, drugging, and eventual miraculous recovery, including my escape from the South Tower of the World Trade Center on 9/11. More importantly, it's the story of the gifts and miracles I have experienced as a result of living in Step Twelve, gleaned from many years of active service for home groups, intergroups, clubhouses, and roundups; from travelling North America performing the role of Bill W. in national tours of the live stage production *Pass It On . . . An Evening with Bill W. & Dr. Bob;* and from serving as a Twelve Step advocate and as a circuit speaker at meetings, conferences, workshops, conventions, schools, hospitals, jails, military installations, rehabs, halfway houses, drug courts, and DUI courts from coast to coast in the United States and Canada.

In part 2, I tell the story of the beginnings of AA through the first three Twelfth Step calls: Ebby Thatcher's visit with Bill W., Bill W.'s visit with Dr. Bob, and Bill and Bob's visit with AA number three, Billy D. I also explore the maturation of the Twelve Step program under the guidance of the early members who made the Twelfth Step call the keystone in the evolution and growth of AA, saving millions of lives worldwide and serving as the model for dozens of Twelve Step programs that reach people with addictions to everything from heroin to gambling, as well as their family members, through Al-Anon and Nar-Anon.

Part 3 includes information on how to conduct a Twelfth Step call (and overcome barriers to service work unique to the twenty-first century); the importance of sponsorship as a necessary requirement for working Step Twelve; why Step Twelve is the holy grail of recovery, the culmination of working all of the preceding eleven Steps; and a discussion about the vital importance of living a life of service beyond helping alcoholics and addicts.

Part 4 is devoted to testimonials from Step Twelve warriors who have dedicated themselves to a life of service. Stories of recovering people are also sprinkled throughout the book to show, rather than just tell, how these ideas and principles are put into practice in the myriad ways that reflect the amazing variety of people in Twelve Step programs.

Twelfth Step work has become my mission in life: my passion, avocation, and vocation. The glue that holds me together. Twelfth Step and service work beyond the program brings me a quality of unspeakable joy and a peace that passes all understanding as it saves my life over and over again.

In the words of Bill W.: "Sobriety is . . . only the first gift of the first awakening. If more gifts are to be received, our awakening has to go on." (Bill W., December 1957)

I am on fire with the desire to pass on to others my passion for Step Twelve—the key to the kingdom of life beyond our wildest dreams.

PART 1

My Story

❦

. . . in which I cheat death, return from the gates of the hell
of addiction, and find the spiritual solution in the
Twelve Step program that allowed me to live a life of
service in Step Twelve

1

What It Was Like

Having had a spiritual awakening as a result of working all twelve of the Steps, we are compelled to carry our message to those who still suffer, passing on to others the gift that was freely given to us.

We carry the message that we have found a spiritual solution to our common problem and then we pass on our knowledge of the Twelve Steps, which leads us to the spiritual solution.

The first weapon in our Step Twelve tool kit is sharing our personal stories of drinking and recovery. Often when we tell our stories to a sick and suffering friend, it is the first time they have ever heard someone speaking from personal experience about what they have been going through and carrying the good news that we have found the way out. Through sharing our own experience, strength, and hope, we gain their confidence, they come to trust us, and they listen to what we have to say.

As Dr. Bob describes his first encounter with Bill W., "He was the first living human with whom I had ever talked, who knew what he was talking about in regard to alcoholism from actual experience. In other words, he talked my language. He knew all the answers, and certainly not because he had picked them up in his reading." (*Alcoholics Anonymous* 2001, 180)

This is my story—to the best of my recollection. If anyone has more accurate information as to my whereabouts between 1978 and 1998, please let me know. I was in a blackout for most of those twenty years.

I don't know if I was born an alcoholic, but I sure could have used a drink the first day of kindergarten.

My name is Gary K. and I am a recovered alcoholic and drug addict, formerly of the hopeless, demoralized variety. I don't have all the answers, but I can tell you with certainty that the answers will come when you walk the talk, do the work that is yours to do, and get your own house in order.

As a direct result of turning my life over to the care of God, clearing away the wreckage of the past, living in Step Twelve, sponsoring others, volunteering for service, and surrounding myself with the loving wall of humanity that I find in the various Twelve Step fellowships to which I belong, it has not been necessary for me to take a drink or a drug since August 25, 1998. Twelve Step recovery has given me an extraordinary life, and for that I am forever grateful.

Today I am happy, joyous, and free from alcohol, pot, poppers, hashish, opium, cocaine, Percodan, Percocet, Vicodin, ketamine, Quaaludes, morphine, IV heroin, and crack. I am also a recovering sex addict, debtor, and overeater.

I grew up in Canton, Ohio, just south of Akron, the birthplace of Twelve Step recovery. It was in Akron, just blocks from Dr. Bob's house, that a police officer stood on my face for the very first time during a drunk driving incident.

I arrived on this planet kicking and screaming on November 7, 1960, the day John F. Kennedy was elected president. I was so terrified of being alive and trapped in a body that I didn't talk for three years. When I finally spoke, my first word was "pocketbook" and my father remarked, "Whatever that means, it can't be good."

My name at birth was William Joseph Weaver Jr.—or "Bill W." as my sponsor once pointed out—which may offer some explanation as to why I have become a fervent Twelve Step evangelist.

My birth parents were uneducated, illiterate alcoholics. There was constant domestic violence in the home of my birth. At the age of one, God did for me what I could not do for myself—I was rescued by Child Protective Services and spared from living life as Billy Joe Weaver. The authorities turned me over to the care of Reverend Foreman, a Methodist minister, who placed me into the loving adoptive home of a saintly couple, Bruce and Mary Evelyn, who gave me my current surname.

Bruce and Mary Evelyn met during their freshman year of high school in 1939 and continued dating all through World War II, even when Bruce was overseas serving on the underwater demolition team for the U.S. Navy. Neither of them ever dated anyone else, and they never spent a night apart during their sixty-plus years of marriage. Never once did they raise their voices in anger—not to one another or to anyone else.

From the day World War II ended until the day they died in their eighties, every Friday night they played cards with the same group of friends, ate pizza, drank Coca Cola, and laughed until the wee hours. They didn't drink, didn't smoke, didn't gossip, and wouldn't say shit if they had a mouthful of it. They were kind, hard-working, and loyal; they loved God. And they both volunteered for service in the community, at the schools I attended, and at their church where they never missed a Sunday service. Bruce was an honest used car salesman, football fan, and avid golfer. Mary Evelyn was a stay-at-home mother, a painter, and a poet.

They intuitively and naturally lived the spiritual principles of the Twelve Steps without ever needing to read the Big Book.

I also had an adopted sister who had different birth parents. She grew up as normal as one could be. As an adult, she held down the same job for many years; entered into a healthy, stable marriage; became a wonderful mother; and raised two remarkable children. She could take a drink or leave it.

My sister and I were raised by the same loving parents, with the same values, in the same spiritually driven household, but unlike my sister I was born with a potentially fatal, progressive disease of mind, body, and spirit—a kind of brain disorder that coaxed me from our idyllic, wholesome, loving home and led me down a dark, twisted road to a life of terrifying depravity, insanity, and demoralization, ultimately depositing me at the gates of death.

I am living proof that, rather than being a moral failing, addiction is a disease—just like cancer or diabetes or tuberculosis, addiction and alcoholism are diseases. The disease doesn't care where we were raised, who raised us, what side of the tracks we grew up on, how much money or education we did or didn't have, what color our skin is, or whether or not we were raised with spiritual guidance.

I was born without an ENOUGH button and with my MORE button stuck in the "on" position. The disease of MORE began to manifest when I was ten years old. I developed my first obsessive ritual that involved my childhood "drugs" of choice: sugar, carbs, fear, and fantasy. Each day after school, I would walk in the house, drop my books, and head for the kitchen. From the cupboard, I would grab my favorite quart-sized green glass tumbler, fill it half full with milk, and then add half a box of Nestlé's Quik, creating chocolate milk as thick as split pea soup that was positively buzzing with sugar.

Armed with my tumbler of sugar and a box of cherry sparkle Pop-Tarts, I would race to the TV room to lose myself in tales of werewolves, vampires, and Hollywood divas on my two favorite programs—*Dark Shadows* and *The Merv Griffin Show.* After gorging on Pop-Tarts and guzzling my sugary chocolate goo, I would pass out on the couch before it was time for dinner.

This was addiction and alcoholism manifesting in my life before I ever met booze or drugs.

When I was nine, my parents would occasionally arrange for me to spend the weekend with another family who lived on a farm. Both of my parents had grown up in rural areas and thought the outdoor activity would be good for me. During each of these weekends, I was repeatedly molested. I did not know how to ask for help—afraid to tell on the perpetrator and too ashamed to tell my parents. This continued until I was nearly twelve years old. I do not believe for a moment that the childhood abuse I suffered turned me into an alcoholic, but it did throw emotional gasoline on a fearful fire that had started burning the day I was born.

My father was a huge football fan. The Pro Football Hall of Fame is in Canton, Ohio, and each year there is a parade held during the NFL kickoff game. My father was in charge of lining up convertible automobiles for the parade. For this service he would receive gifts from the Hall of Fame Board of Trustees. One year they presented him with a souvenir porcelain decanter, formed in the shape of the Football Hall of Fame and containing eighty-year-old Jim Beam whiskey.

Bruce kept this bottle in a place of honor in our home. He had no interest in what was inside of that bottle. No one in our family drank and none of my parents' friends drank, so as a child I had absolutely no exposure to alcohol—even at the church we attended they used grape juice when serving communion. And yet, from the day that bottle arrived in our house, I was captivated by the allure of that whiskey decanter. Somehow, I always knew that I was destined to have a relationship with the elixir inside of that bottle and dreamed of the day that I would break the seal and meet King Alcohol.

When I was thirteen, I had a growth spurt and my voice changed. One weekend my parents announced that they were going to leave me at the farm for the weekend and pick me up Sunday evening. I summoned every ounce of courage I could muster and begged them to allow me to stay home alone. After all, I was a good kid and well behaved, very smart, very capable, and could certainly take care of myself. They agreed. At last, this was my chance!

Bruce must have noticed me staring at that bottle. He was missing a finger from one hand as a result of an accident, and just before walking out of the house and leaving me alone for the week-end, he referred to his four-fingered hand as "hospital" and the five-fingered hand as "sudden death" and promised that I would receive them both if I dared to open that bottle of whiskey. I swore a solemn oath, but the minute their car disappeared down the street, I made a beeline for that bottle. I filled a teakettle with water to make a head of steam, which I used to loosen the glue, and carefully removed the seal from my father's precious Hall of Fame whiskey decanter—a trick I learned from watching *I Love Lucy.* I popped the cork and took my very first drink of liquid courage. I felt powerful for the first time in my life. Fears vanished. I drank every drop of that whiskey and spent much of that weekend running around naked. I experienced the most awesome weekend of my life. I felt so invincible that I beat up a neighborhood bully who had picked on me.

Before my parents returned, I filled the decanter with water, replaced the cork, reattached the seal, and returned it to its place of honor, where it remained until my father passed away many years later. (On his deathbed, as I made my final amends, my father told me that he always knew I had drunk the whiskey and filled the bottle with water—I had put the seal on upside down!)

From that day forward I was madly in love with booze.

Fortunately for my love affair, we had many Italian families in our neighborhood, and they all produced homemade wine and grappa, which I would steal and hide inside the paneled walls of my basement bedroom. While my family was asleep, I would drink the night away, watching old movies on the black-and-white TV in my bedroom, dreaming of becoming an actor. Often I would call a taxi service, give them a neighbor's address, climb out of the window, go there to catch the cab, and sneak off to local bars—I was tall and no one ever carded me. It was the mid-1970s, and my favorite sport became getting hammered in discos and stripping while I danced.

I acted in all of the school plays and musicals and showed talent. My parents enrolled me in acting classes at our local community theater where I began performing with semiprofessional actors. I developed a passion for escaping from myself by becoming a character in a play. I excelled and I was hooked. I desperately wanted to be anyone but me and became a fairly skilled young actor. Everyone encouraged me to continue pursuing this dream.

When I turned sixteen years old, I earned my driver's license. The very next day, before driving myself to school, I drank four bottles of wine, went into a blackout, and became involved in a serious automobile accident. Two people were critically injured and later died as a result. The emotional consequences were devastating for everyone touched by this tragedy. Though the police were unable to clearly determine who was at fault, I was tortured with guilt. My drinking rapidly escalated, and by the time I graduated high school I had totaled eleven automobiles. One day Bruce came to me and said, "Son, your drinking has caused mayhem and injured others, and you have totaled eleven cars, your mother and I want you to find a college in New York City so that you won't have to drive."

A stroke of genius! By then, I knew I had a drinking problem, and my father had come up with a brilliant solution—taxis and subways.

At the age of seventeen, at 2:00 a.m. on the day I graduated from high school, with $5,000 cash in my pocket, I boarded the Amtrak train headed for New York City to attend school at The American Academy of Dramatic Arts, an acting conservatory that held classes from 2:00 p.m. to 6:00 p.m. They included dancing, fencing, scene study, and vocal training—requiring only four hours of study each day. This was the perfect curriculum for a practicing alcoholic, and I figured I could get smashed every night and always make it to class on time.

My first day in New York City, I talked my way into an apartment in Times Square. On my second day, I happened to walk past a store that sold outlandish costumes, where I purchased a large straw farmer's hat, a pair of oversized sunglasses, a pair of gold lamé Daisy Dukes, and a red ostrich feather boa. That evening—shirtless, wearing my gold lamé shorts, farmer's hat, sunglasses, and boa—

I made a beeline for Studio 54, the infamous headquarters of artist Andy Warhol and his wild band of glitterati and hangers-on. If you wanted to gain entrance, the doorman had to like you and you had to be very famous, very sexy, or very odd. Being a half-naked seventeen-year-old wearing a red feather boa and a pair of tight, gold lamé shorts did the trick, so I sashayed into the most famous disco in the world. I had arrived: I was going to take New York by storm. That night I got plastered, snorted coke in a private room filled with celebrities, and eventually stripped butt naked on the dance floor. I was offered a job.

After a week of shaking my ass at Studio 54, I landed stripping jobs at other night spots. Drugs and liquor are expensive, and my $5,000 cash scholarship was quickly disappearing, along with what was left of my morals. Someone suggested that I could earn big bucks as a male prostitute. I was waking up every morning with coyote-ugly strangers in bed next to me anyway, so it seemed like a good idea. For the next two years, I drank, drugged, stripped, and prostituted myself—and in my spare time, I studied acting and attended Broadway plays and musicals.

Through a friend from school, I learned about an audition for a replacement dancer in the musical, *The Best Little Whorehouse in Texas.* They were looking for young men willing to dance in their jock straps on stage. For me this was a no-brainer. I got the part and so began my career in professional New York theater. From the age of twenty until my mid-thirties, I drank and drugged my way around the world, touring in Broadway musicals and plays in regional theaters and off Broadway.

Show business was a perfect enabler for my disease. I was surrounded by other drunks and drug fiends, and we only had to work two hours a day.

Talented, quirky, and too tall for the chorus, I always landed leading character roles. Many of the promoters knew that I was a drug addict, and it was typical for me to arrive at a theater, walk into my dressing room, and find gifts on my makeup table such as a fifth of Jack Daniels, a large fruit basket, and an eight ball of cocaine, with a lovely welcoming note. I would always think, "What's up with that fruit basket?"

I began injecting heroin into the veins in my neck just for the sport and drama of it, and became unbearable to work with. I was mad as a hatter: angry, violent, and verbally abusive. It had become common knowledge that I was a junkie and was always drunk, but I continued to garner rave reviews and standing ovations.

Heroin had become a staple in my daily drug regimen, which would cause me to projectile vomit at the most inconvenient times and without warning. I had been portraying the role of Daddy Warbucks for several years on world tours and in multiple productions. I was up for the role in the Broadway revival, and one evening, during a benefit performance raising money for AIDS charities— the audience filled with celebrities, dignitaries, and a national press corps—I vomited all over Little Orphan Annie on stage in front of everyone.

That was the end of my theater career for many years.

Unable to find work, I began to deal drugs and discovered crack cocaine, which was the express train to my bottom. I became completely unemployable. My sanity had flown the coop—I became desperate and began robbing apartments, mugging people, and stealing from my friends. I lived with someone I loved dearly who was dying from AIDS, and I began to steal his morphine. When he passed away, I found myself completely and utterly alone.

I began to beg God to let me die in my sleep. One evening while heading out to meet a drug dealer before going to a nightclub to drink, I found a prayer card lying on the sidewalk. On one side was an image of St. Michael and this prayer: "St. Michael the Archangel, defend us in battle. Be our protection against the wickedness and snares of the Devil. May God rebuke him, we humbly pray, and do thou O Prince of the Heavenly hosts, by the power of God, thrust into Hell Satan, and all the evil spirits, who prowl about the world seeking the ruin of souls. Amen." That evening I began to

obsessively repeat the St. Michael prayer aloud, over and over as I
knocked back several rounds of whiskey.

Two days later, I came to from a blackout during a rainstorm
in the middle of the night, curled up in a ball under the protection
of a massive sculpture. When I opened my eyes, I was greeted by
a view of a severed head, which was part of a statue of St. Michael
having just slain the devil.

I was confused, frightened, shaking badly, and began to cry and
howl like a wounded animal. I didn't know where I was or how I
got there. I was awake inside of a nightmare that had become real.
The last thing that I could remember was fighting with someone
near Battery Park in lower Manhattan. As I took in my present circumstances, in shock and horror, I began shouting "Where are my
shoes? Where is my wallet? Where in hell am I?!"

A kind priest was just returning to the rectory in the driving
rain, heard my caterwauling, and found me looking like a bum,
shivering, soaking wet, and muddy. He approached me with no fear
and asked if I was hurt.

He wanted to check me into their men's shelter. I had severe
shakes and was still fairly incoherent from booze and pills, but I
assured him that I had an apartment. I told him that I had lost my
wallet and that I just needed to get warm, dry off, and figure out
a way to get home. He asked me if I needed to eat something or
maybe have some coffee. He suggested that we get out of the rain
and he would find me something dry to wear home.

The priest escorted me into a men's shelter in the basement of
a massive church. He handed me a pair of sweatpants, a sweatshirt,
a buttered bagel, and a cup of coffee. For what seemed like an eter-
nity, he talked to me about Twelve Step recovery and AA while I ate.
He then gave me ten dollars, said a prayer, and made me promise
to come to church and visit him again one day. I asked him the
location of this church and he said, "Morningside Heights, 112th
and Amsterdam Avenue."

The rain had let up some, and I caught a taxi home. I had left without knowing the name of the priest or the name of the church. It was difficult to see any details of the exterior of the church due to my condition, the dark of night, and the driving rain. All that I could discern was that it was a massive, spooky, monolithic Gothic structure. I began having recurring night terrors involving that sculpture of St. Michael, the devil's severed head, the big spooky church, and the old priest.

Within a week, I hit the first of several painful bottoms and became suicidal with depression. I'd heard about the Carrier Clinic addiction treatment center, so I phoned a social worker at the Actors Fund of America and made plans for my first rehab experience—an eighteen-day stay.

It was during rehab that I attended my first AA meeting and heard the message. It was in rehab that I learned that I was suffering from a disease and not a moral weakness.

Upon discharge, I rode the train back to New York City alone. I walked into my apartment, dropped my bags, phoned a drug dealer, and called the liquor store. Once again, I was off to the races on another epic spree, which lasted several weeks. I was mentally incapable of leaving my apartment except to get drugs and food. I had a pit bull named Amanda and had become incapable of taking her outside. There was dog crap all over the floors, garbage piled high, bugs and rats everywhere—my once gorgeous apartment had become a squalid nightmare.

An old friend had seen me stumbling through the streets and reached out to me. He told me that a former acting student of mine was in recovery. He gave me her phone number and suggested that I call on her. But before I had the chance to phone her, she called me and told me she would come by the following afternoon to talk to me about my drinking. I thought, "Uh-oh. The jig is up. People know. People are talking. She is going to see the mess and there will be no turning back."

So naturally that night I went on a rip-roaring bender—shooting up heroin, drinking, and smoking crack—and fell asleep naked in the middle of my living room.

The next afternoon, my former student Veronica M. and a man who identified himself as Charlie M. opened my unlocked front door and found me in a heap on the floor. I was sweaty, filthy, bruised from head to toe, unshaven, unwashed, had swollen lips and puke on my clothes, and was lying in dog shit.

I was mortified. It was bad enough that my former student had to see me in this condition, but who is this guy with her? She explained that this is called a Twelfth Step call from AA and they always show up in pairs. They were both clean and shiny, too peaceful, and too goddamn happy. They spent time qualifying, telling me their stories of recovery. They explained to me that they had a spiritual tool kit that held the solution to my problem.

Veronica cried with me. She leaned down and kissed my forehead. She told me that this was my Via Dolorosa—the road to transformation and resurrection. I had no idea what the fuck she was talking about. She asked if I wanted what she had. Sure I did— if what she had was a sandwich, a bottle of Scotch, a pack of cigarettes, and a hundred bucks to get more crack. She whispered to me, "Do you want to get sober?" I grumbled and nodded. She asked "Are you willing to go to any lengths?" and again I nodded. She asked if I had a bucket and scrub brush. I mumbled and pointed to the kitchen. She returned with a bucket of soapy water, placed the scrub brush in my hand, and said, "First things first. Scrub the dog shit off the floor—welcome to sobriety!"

An eviction notice had been delivered by the landlord and was posted on my front door. Veronica and Charlie proceeded to help me divest myself of my worldly belongings. The two of them watched and gave their moral support as I accepted responsibility for the mess, hauling out garbage bag after garbage bag, carts filled with books, and broken furniture. They guided me as I attempted to restore the apartment to sanitary.

Veronica and Charlie agreed to store a few boxes for me, so they packed up my family photos, theater memorabilia, and some clothing—including a tuxedo I had tailor-made for me to wear to the Tony Awards. Veronica suggested that I hang on to the tuxedo in case I needed to find employment as a waiter. On the anniversary of my first year of sobriety, one of the miracles that are commonplace in this fellowship of the spirit took place. I was invited to the black-tie "Bill W. Dinner Dance," a fundraiser for New York Intergroup being held at the Marriott Marquis Hotel. I wore the tuxedo that Veronica and Charlie had saved for me. They were both also at the dinner.

The following morning, I made my second trip to a New Jersey rehab. After a stay of ninety days I was discharged. Determined to make it this time, I stayed at the home of my roommate from the treatment center. Together we went to meetings for a few weeks. Several men offered to sponsor me and take me through the Steps. I felt I had this thing licked, and yet, the only word I could see in the Steps was the word GOD, and I just couldn't stomach it. After a couple weeks, I stopped attending my outpatient groups and Twelve Step meetings, and before long I was calling the liquor store and the drug dealers for delivery and began the descent to my final horrific bottom.

2

What Happened

❦

My health, my sanity, and my morality had hit unimaginable lows. I looked like Charles Manson on a starvation diet.

After a week-long blackout bender, I woke up in the middle of the night in a park in Forest Hills, Queens. I was lying in a mud puddle: naked, broken rib, broken sternum, stab wounds, face badly cut, teeth knocked out, broken jaw, mouth full of pieces of a broken crack pipe, and covered from head to toe with human feces. Someone had beaten me and left me for dead. I was bleeding badly but managed to drag myself out to the street.

The area was deserted. I stood alone in the middle of the street shouting at God or whoever was listening. "I am not a monster! I was in Broadway musicals. Please help me, please God, please help me!!"

In the distance headlights appeared. A taxi approached. The driver rolled down his window, staring at me, shaking his head with a look of pity on his face. He asked me if I was a drug addict, and I said yes. He asked me if I was high, and I said no, but I need something.

He told me that he knew exactly what I was going through—he had been there himself. He took a blanket out of the trunk and wrapped it around me. He tried to talk me into going to the hospital, but I told him I wanted to go home and he agreed to drive me there. As he drove, he told me about AA, CA (Cocaine Anonymous), and NA (Narcotics Anonymous). He told me about the meetings he attended. He told me that there was a spiritual solution to my problem and that it worked. As I got out of his taxi, he offered to give me his copy of the NA Big Book. I declined his offer, though in the deepest part of my soul I knew that he was talking Truth with a capital *T*. I never saw him again, but I know he was yet another recovery angel, a spiritual warrior carrying the message to me in my darkest hour.

With no keys, naked, stinking to high heaven, bleeding, and in great pain, I managed to break into my own apartment. I wanted the pain to go away. I knew I had crack pipes to scrape and bottles with backwash strewn all over my apartment. Hoping I might have a can of beer, I opened the fridge. It was empty except for a carton of milk. I hadn't eaten in many days; I grabbed the carton and in a single gulp downed the contents. It was spoiled rotten.

I began to wretch and threw up amber liquid into the sink. The amber liquid smelled like Jack Daniels and was full of white lumps of curdled milk. In my drug-induced psychotic state, the white lumps looked like pieces of crack. Not wanting to waste the booze, I began lapping up my vomit. I patted off the little white lumps into a paper towel and proceeded to try to smoke my puke.

When that didn't work, I knew I had really had it. I was done— done living. On an earlier dark night of the soul, I had created a suicide kit—a mason jar full of Vicodin, which I saved for a rainy day and hid in the back of my closet. This was that rainy day. I proceeded to swallow them all and curled up on the floor prepared to leave this dense plane.

Suddenly my mind was flooded with thoughts about an actor I had worked with on the world tour of *My Fair Lady*. He was always kind to me. He played Colonel Pickering to my Henry Higgins. Though I had not spoken to him in a couple of years, I remembered his phone number and crawled to the telephone. In a very weak voice, I muttered "Colonel—help me. Help me." By the time he reached my apartment, I was unconscious. He managed to get me into his car and then to detox and my final trip to rehab. Unbeknownst to me, my friend had been sober for over a decade, and though at that time I didn't quite believe in God, clearly God believed in me. (This was 1998, and twelve years later that same actor who saved my life would play Dr. Bob to my Bill W. in the national tour of the off-Broadway play *Bill W. and Dr. Bob,* including at the seventy-fifth international AA convention. He later went on to travel with me, playing Dr. Bob in dozens of cities throughout North America, carrying the message through the national tours of *Pass It On . . . An Evening with Bill W. & Dr. Bob,* which he helped me to produce. How can we not believe in miracles?)

I came to in another rehab in New Jersey, for another ninety days. I was ready this time. I began to devour the literature, studying the Big Book letter and verse, and reading and rereading the Twelve and Twelve. I wanted it. I wanted it badly. I felt that I had truly surrendered.

Each morning and evening, AA groups from New York City and various groups in New Jersey brought meetings into the rehab. They always showed up early and stayed long after the meeting to talk with anyone who was interested in what they had to offer. The day I was discharged from what would be my last stay in a rehab facility, one of those AA Twelve Steppers travelled two hours by train from Manhattan to Hopewell, New Jersey, so that he could be at the door of the treatment facility to extend his hand and shepherd me into the rooms and the fellowship. To me he was a saint. He had over forty years of sobriety and became one of my sponsors. His father had been a member of Bill W.'s first AA group on Clinton Street in Brooklyn Heights.

I was staying in the home of my actor friend—"the Colonel," the man who had saved my life during my last bottom. I was told to attend meetings morning, noon, and night. He gave me three dollars every day, figuring I couldn't get in too much trouble with so little money.

Each evening, before attending my home group and sharing my day count, I would sneak over to West Forty-Ninth Street in Hell's Kitchen and buy one big fat joint and smoke it while sitting on the steps of a brownstone. I would then walk around the block, gather my composure, and attend the evening meeting where I would announce my day count: "My name is Gary and I have one day sober . . . two days sober . . . three days sober" and so on. After the meeting I would meet with one of my sponsors, study the Big Book, and continue with Step work.

What I didn't know was that each day, as I sat on the stoop of the brownstone smoking pot before the meeting, I was being watched from a window by the chairperson of my home group who happened to live there. Apparently, most everyone in the meeting knew that I was getting high but no one called me on it. After all, I wasn't drinking alcohol, and the literature mentioned nothing about smoking pot.

My sponsors continued taking me through the Steps while I secretly smoked pot, attended meetings, and announced my daily sobriety count. These dedicated, no-nonsense, tough-love warriors quickly took me through all Twelve Steps within my first thirty days of sobriety. One of those sponsors, Shawn M., took me through Steps Four through Eight during a single weekend.

While working the Fourth Step, I experienced a radical shift in my thinking. I realized that I was not a victim in my life—I had created the mess that I was in. I now knew that everyone I resented had tried to love me, and I had made it impossible for them to do so because I had become incapable of giving or receiving love. My heart was opening up. Remarkable mini miracles were happening around me almost daily. The scales were falling from my eyes.

On my ninetieth day, I got particularly toasted before heading to the meeting. I knew that neither of my sponsors would be able to attend that night so I planned to sit in the back of the room with my eyes closed. I walked into the meeting and discovered that the group had a cake for me. They were going to give me a ninety-day coin and then take me out to dinner. When the meeting began, they read from chapter 5 of the Big Book: "Rarely have we seen a person fail who has thoroughly followed our path. Those who do not recover are people who cannot or will not completely give themselves to this simple program, usually men and women who are constitutionally incapable of being honest with themselves."

That passage pierced my heart like a hot knife. I burst into tears and confessed to the group that I had been smoking pot. As I sobbed uncontrollably, my new friends in my home group cheered me on as I ratted out my disease. That was August 25, 1998, and I have stayed clean since that day. I had learned to tell on my disease. (Although, it was not until several weeks later that I found the courage to tell my sponsors that I had been smoking pot during my first ninety days.) I vowed to wage a holy war against alcoholism and addiction. I became so angry at the disease that had lied to me, took away everything that I previously cherished about life, and then tried to kill me.

My sponsors, Edgar W. and Shawn M., both old-time, tough love fundamentalists, patiently shadowed my every move for many months during my early recovery. They told me that whatever happened in New York City after sundown was none of my business and that I should not go outside alone without adult supervision.

They showed me how to laugh again, told me the truth, armed me with recovery literature, bought me clothing, and took me to church. They helped me find a job, a doctor, a dentist, a lawyer, and a therapist; supplied me with friends and coffee; fed me prayers, slogans, and hamburgers; and located sofas for me to crash on.

They impressed upon me that we are taught the Big Book letter and verse and taken through the Steps so that we are able to pass our knowledge on to others and help them achieve sobriety, ultimately ensuring a continued and quality sobriety for ourselves. They promised me that service work would be the beginning of the end of isolation and that this Step work would set me free from the bondage of selfishness, guilt, shame, and remorse.

They required me to sign up for an array of opportunities to carry the message and practice the art of the Twelfth Step call by answering the phones at New York Intergroup and accompanying my sponsors on Twelfth Step calls to private homes, sanitariums, detox wards, jails, and hospitals.

My sponsors arranged for me to share my experience, strength, and hope by telling my story at dozens of Twelve Step meetings all over the five boroughs of New York City, accompanying me to each meeting in order to lend their moral support. They both insisted that I volunteer for service commitments at each meeting that I attended, including setting up chairs, cleaning ashtrays, making coffee, and arriving thirty minutes before each meeting started so that I could stand at the door to welcome and shake the hand of every member who walked into the meeting room.

Some of us are sicker than others, and I was sicker than most. So, very shortly after my ninetieth day sober—and just a few days off of my marijuana maintenance program—I got busy and found my first pigeon. Mercifully, God took good care of both of us. He stayed sober, and that sponsorship experience changed my life. Looking back through my current sober lenses, I realize that I should have quickly confessed my pot smoking to my sponsors and started a new day count before attempting to become a sponsor. On the other hand, only a few days after Dr. Bob took his last drink on June 10, 1935 he said to Bill W., "if we are going to stay sober we had better get busy." On June 26 Bill W. and Dr. Bob met "the man in the bed," AA number 3, Billy Dotson. On July 4, 1935 Bill W. and Dr. Bob became Billy D.'s sponsors. Bill W. had been sober for 6 months and Dr. Bob had only 24 days since his last drink. Right out of the gate, with very little sobriety, they got busy working intensively with others. This allowed them to remain happy, joyous, and free of booze and drugs. That was also my experience.

During my first year of sobriety, I walked more than a dozen men through the Twelve Steps. I don't know if I was a good sponsor for those guys, but working with them kept me sober. Since my first year of sobriety, I have taken more than two hundred men through the Twelve Steps, for which I have received priceless rewards. While sponsorship is sometimes a pain in the ass, I do it anyway: Passing on the gift of sobriety is what keeps me sober and drug-free. To be unwilling to take the time to give away that which was freely given to me would be a supreme act of selfishness, and selfishness is the root of our troubles. The more Twelfth Step work I do, the more I am aware of undeniable miracles manifesting in, around, and through my life on a daily basis.

At six months truly clean and sober, I had been spending most of my time doing Step Twelve service, working only odd jobs for members of the fellowship—walking dogs, running errands, and cleaning apartments. The time had come to find a decent sobriety gig to pay the bills while I continued to clean up my side of the street and expand my God consciousness through Step Twelve service.

A new friend I had met at a Twelve Step meeting invited me to stay with him until I could find a full-time job. I had no money and no food in my empty apartment. I was comforted by his companionship, and his refrigerator and cupboards were full of food.

On my first Sunday morning there, my friend arose early to make us breakfast. He told me that we were going to attend services at his home church. I hadn't been inside a church since I left Ohio when I was seventeen. I grew up in church and my paternal grandfather had been a minister, which brought to mind a passage in the Big Book that states that having had a spiritual awakening, many of us return to our religious roots. Still, I was tired that morning—my friend and I had stayed up very late talking about the Big Book and the Steps—and I wanted to sleep in. But I had developed the habit of practicing Step Three on a daily basis—turning my life and my will over to the care of the God that I now experienced but didn't understand. I was completely on board with the promise that astonishing things would continue to happen when I got out of the way, so I quickly dressed for church services.

When our taxi turned east off of Broadway at 112th Street and I saw the massive cathedral come into view, my heart began to race. I was experiencing intense déjà vu as I saw the enormous sculpture of St. Michael and the severed head of the devil. I became extremely excited—my goose bumps had goose bumps. Jabbering like a monkey, I regaled my friend with memories of my experience waking up in the rain under that statue of St. Michael, as well as the old priest and the nightmares.

As we entered the great cathedral and slowly walked up the nave, I was awestruck by the dark beauty of the magnificent sanctuary. I chose a seat in the front row, an aisle seat on the right side.

Suddenly the service started, and the entire congregation stood and faced the back of the nave. The massive pipe organ was booming the processional hymn as the procession slowly made its way up the nave toward the great choir and the high altar: the priests in their robes, the adult choir, the children's choir, the acolytes, smoke billowing from the thurible with the smell of frankincense. Memories of childhood came flooding back, and I began to tremble as healing tears of joy rolled down my face.

As the cross passed by, the congregants would gently bow their heads as if Christ himself were walking past. As the cross reached the front row where I was standing, I glanced at the priest at the head of the procession and saw that it was the priest who had helped me on that dark rainy night over a year ago when I was about to hit my first bottom!

I stared at him, and he looked right into my eyes. I saw the look of recognition come across his face. He beamed a joyful smile and began to nod his head; I bowed mine and burst into tears. I felt a tingling sensation in the top of my head, as if heavenly fingers were massaging my brain. I have never felt so loved.

I knew in my heart of hearts that the circumstances that led me back to this cathedral were not mere coincidences. Through God's grace and mercy, I now had four spiritual homes—three Twelve Step fellowships and the Cathedral of St. John the Divine.

———

Several members of our congregation were also in recovery. One of them owned an office temp agency. She taught me how to type and use various office-related computer programs, and began sending me out on office temp assignments.

Every Sunday I attended both 9:00 and 11:00 a.m. services, as well as evening Vespers. Week after week, I would spend every Sunday from early morning until well after sundown inside the massive, magnificent cathedral. I polished silver, did cleaning, and helped with coffee hour. I became a greeter and an acolyte. I was learning to practice our spiritual principles in all of my affairs. My life was beginning to stabilize: I was becoming a respected member of the community.

The temp agency sent me to a prominent Wall Street brokerage firm. I was assigned to a high-level executive with twenty years of sobriety. She hadn't been to a meeting in two years and was no longer actively working her program. Within my first week of employment, she relapsed right in front of me, resulting in a Jekyll-and-Hyde personality change where she became verbally abusive. Yet, with only a few months of sobriety under my belt, I took care of her that day and guided her out of the offices and into the rooms of recovery, urging her to pocket her pride and restart her program. At the end of the day, she cancelled my assignment and sent me off with six months of wages. She then flew to the Betty Ford Center in California.

When she returned from treatment, she phoned me to work her Ninth Step and make amends. She told me I had grace under pressure, and she offered me a job with the firm. As a direct result of working Step Twelve, I began working for a major Wall Street brokerage house with offices in the World Trade Center.

The bridge back to life was teeming with opportunity and love. I could not deny the direct relationship between daily maintenance of my spiritual condition, serving others, and the manifestation of great events in my life. I was elected as a general service representative, served on roundup steering committees, chaired meetings, helped create sober social events, and was invited to share my story at meetings in several states. I was also elected to the vestry at the Cathedral of St. John the Divine, the governing body of the congregation.

Service became my new drug of choice: I began to discover the significant healing benefits of practicing our spiritual principles outside the rooms of recovery.

Demonstrating my gratitude for this newfound joy of living and the great gifts of my sobriety, each morning upon rising I prayed and asked God to continue increasing my territory for Step Twelve service. And on the morning of 9/11, my prayers were powerfully answered.

On August 25, 2001, my sobriety anniversary, I was diagnosed with a potentially fatal progressive immune system disorder. I travelled from New York City to my boyhood home in Ohio to inform my elderly, long-suffering parents that I had become seriously ill. While en route to Ohio, I broke out with shingles. As my immune system had crashed, a massive eruption of shingles covered my torso, front and back, my neck, and my forehead. I tried to distract myself while in Ohio by attending numerous AA meetings. I was given my three-year anniversary coin while in Ohio.

On September 10, I travelled back to New York City and informed several close friends that my condition could prove fatal. I telephoned a new sponsee to inform him about my medical condition, and that I planned to quit my job and could no longer be his sponsor. He replied "But what about my Fifth Step?" Though I was gravely ill and covered with painful shingles, I agreed to meet my new sponsee the next morning at the World Trade Center to listen to his Fifth Step.

My immune system was severely compromised. I was unable to take the treatment for shingles due to an allergic reaction to the medication, and my health was in rapid decline. Though I was in agony, I was unwilling to take the narcotic pain relievers prescribed—I didn't want to awaken the monster, addiction. I prayed without ceasing, asking God to relieve me of the pain.

Weak as a kitten, on the morning of 9/11, I took the subway to the World Trade Center. To bolster my courage, I held on to my three-year sobriety medallion. My plan was to meet with my sponsee, then quit my job and get my affairs in order.

As we ate breakfast together in the Grand Concourse of the South Tower, the plane hit the North Tower and all hell broke loose. Everyone became panic-stricken. Having been struck by falling debris as they walked outside, badly injured people were rushing back into the building.

On loudspeakers security was asking everyone to go upstairs to their offices. They began to chain the doors shut to protect everyone from falling glass and debris.

There was a recovering alcoholic who worked as a security guard in the South Tower. I knew this guy from the Wall Street meeting. There was a joke around the brokerage firms that whatever he told you to do, if you did the opposite you would be in good shape. On the morning of 9/11, he was three sheets to the wind. He spotted my sponsee and me and warned us, "Whatever you do, don't leave the building." My sponsee looked at me and said, "We gotta get the hell outta here right now!" We both laughed, never imagining that the buildings were going to collapse.

There seemed to be no way out. Thousands of people had the same idea at the same moment: escape the building on the PATH train—the port authority train from New York to New Jersey in the subbasement of the building! Suddenly a swarming, panicked mob of humanity began to shove and scramble down the escalators into the subbasement, all headed for the train.

Through the heroic and valiant efforts of my sponsee, we managed to escape the tower in the last group to leave the building on the last PATH train to New Jersey, just moments before the second plane hit the South Tower.

We made it across the Hudson River to New Jersey, and from the promenade at Exchange Place in New Jersey, directly across the river, we watched as the towers fell. The cloud of debris rapidly headed in our direction.

I was well aware that many of our friends and colleagues had likely just perished when the towers collapsed; my world seemed to be coming to an end. Clearly in shock, I adamantly announced to my sponsee that I would find a liquor store, break in, and get hammered. God bless the newcomer: with only two months of sobriety and only Step Four under his belt, my sponsee served up a spiritual awakening by punching me square in the face and reading me the riot act. He then insisted that we get on our knees in the middle of the street and recite the Third Step prayer:

"God, I offer myself to Thee—to build with me and to do with me as Thou wilt. Relieve me of the bondage of self, that I may better do Thy will. Take away my difficulties, that victory over them may bear witness to those I would help of Thy Power, Thy Love, and Thy Way of life. May I do Thy will always!" (*Alcoholics Anonymous* 2001, 63) When you ask God to use you in service, it's a good idea to fasten your chin strap, particularly if your spiritual house is in order. You will indeed receive your marching orders. Invoking the Third Step prayer set into motion a series of dizzying events that changed my life forever.

As we stood in the middle of the street, in the midst of the chaos, through the dense cloud of debris we saw a pair of high-beam headlights. Driving the vehicle was the priest from St. John the Divine who had comforted me in the rainstorm, Twelfth Stepped me, and become my spiritual advisor. He told us that the military was constructing a massive triage at the water's edge and more clergy were desperately needed to do service. Before I knew it, the priest laid his hands on my head and ordained me. I recall how relieved I felt knowing that I had just become a priest, as I was dying and reasoned that my new status might help me get a better room in heaven. I was then escorted to a triage where I was given a hazmat suit.

So now I am dying, I have shingles, I'm a priest, and I'm wearing a hazmat suit. Life beyond my wildest dreams.

Clergy were being asked to post up in the green tent, which was reserved for ministering to those who were in shock and suffering from fear and confusion. The priest who had just ordained me was familiar with the rooms of recovery and instructed me to do what we do in Twelve Step meetings—comfort those who are suffering and listen to their stories.

An Emergency Medical Services worker came into our tent. He was irritable, restless, and clearly discontented. I asked him if he needed to talk. He told me that he was angry and wanted to get drunk. I told him that I had felt the same way a few hours earlier and shared with him that I am a recovering alcoholic and that my sponsee had stopped me from drinking.

His eyes widened—he told me that he was also a friend of Bill W. and that today was his third sobriety anniversary. He was angry because, for the first time in his life, friends had planned to throw him a party and now he couldn't be there because of the attacks on the World Trade Center. He said he felt so selfish and ashamed that he just wanted to go home. He didn't want to stay and help anyone. He needed to be comforted.

I slowly unzipped my hazmat suit, reached into the pocket of my sweatpants, and pulled out my three-year sobriety medallion. I presented it to my new friend as I sang "Happy Anniversary." We both cried and hugged one another. In the middle of the triage, we recited together the Seventh Step prayer: "My Creator, I am now willing that you should have all of me, good and bad. I pray that you now remove from me every single defect of character which stands in the way of my usefulness to you and my fellows. Grant me strength, as I go out from here, to do your bidding." (*Alcoholics Anonymous* 2001, 76)

During the next three days, as the wounded and bewildered filed through the triage by the tens of thousands, I comforted them, prayed with them, listened to stories of survival, and hugged them.

As they wrapped their arms around me, I could feel the blisters from the shingles popping open and oozing inside my hazmat suit. In short order, the pain in my body was subsiding. I grew stronger and stronger, no longer feeling any ill effects from the malady I had been suffering from.

When at last I was able to return to my home in Manhattan, I removed the hazmat suit and stepped into the shower. As I stood in the water rinsing away the sweat, dried blood, and puss, I discovered that the shingles had scabbed up and washed away. I was completely healed—with no medication and virtually no immune system. Several days later, after new blood tests, I received glorious news from my doctor: my immune system showed astonishing improvement.

This was my Step Twelve miracle. This miracle manifested because there are immutable laws in God's universe, not because I am better than anyone else: I am nothing more than a garden-variety drunk and drug addict. As a direct result of practicing the Twelfth Step with my sponsee on 9/11, my life was spared. Through practicing the Step Twelve principles in all of my affairs—giving of myself completely in service and freely giving love and hope to so many of those who were suffering that terrible day—I was given a gift of grace and experienced a miraculous healing in my body.

Just as the Big Book foretells, I had been rocketed into a fourth dimension of existence, which I had never before even dreamed possible.

3

What It Is Like Now

⚜

Love and service is the holy grail of recovery. It is through living in Step Twelve that we find the most profound healing power. This is not a theory. We live it and give it away to keep it.

As we give love to those who are suffering, we are given more love to give away. And as that love passes through us, we are healed, just as Bill W. and Dr. Bob received relief from the compulsion to drink by working with others and carrying a message of hope.

On 9/11, I learned in a very direct and dramatic way the miraculous transformative healing power that comes from living in Step Twelve and suiting ourselves to be of maximum service to God and everyone around us. It is through this radical commitment to service that we find ourselves standing on the cutting edge of the spiritual evolution of the human race.

On the Sunday afternoon following 9/11, I received a phone call from my friend, the recovering priest. He asked me to serve as an acolyte that evening during Vespers. The great choir was lit by candles. The darkened nave was filled with hundreds of mourners—the families of office workers, firemen, police officers, and other first responders who had perished in the towers.

Moments before it was time to begin the service, as the organ began to play, a group of on-duty New York City police officers entered the cathedral through a side door. They had come there in search of priests who would be willing to accompany them down-town to ground zero to bless their souls and their equipment as they prepared to enter the smoldering pit.

They were all visibly shaken.

I was told by the celebrant priest that all clergy were going to ground zero. He asked me to preside over this Vespers service and read the Gospel lessons from the Bible at the high altar. He handed me his homily written on two file cards, patted me on the back, made the sign of the cross, and bolted out the door.

What a strange universe this is! I was once a crack whore and a falling-down drunk crawling around in dog poop. As a result of working the Steps and following God's direction, that night I was called for service at the great cathedral that served our city as a beacon of hope and an international symbol of peace.

When it came time to read the first lesson, I stepped up to the lectern and took in the sight of the massive candlelit cathedral crowded with 9/11 mourners. I looked at my hands resting on the massive Bible, my arms draped with the sleeves of my gleaming white acolyte robe. I thought about where I had been just three years earlier, on my darkest night in that park in Forest Hills, Queens, and there I stood at the high altar of the world's largest cathedral, providing comfort for sick and suffering fellow New Yorkers on a day of national mourning. I opened the Good Book and discovered that the first Gospel lesson was 1 Timothy 1:12–14. Tears of gratitude streamed down my face as I read aloud:

> I thank God, who has given me strength, that He considered me trustworthy, appointing me to His service. Even though I was once a blasphemer, a persecutor, a violent man, and a drunkard *(my addition)*, I was shown mercy because I acted in ignorance and unbelief.

With the certainty of experience, I tell you that if our relationship with God is right, great events will indeed come to pass.

God now had my undivided attention. I began to rely on miracles to get me through each day. I made a commitment to ramp up my service work, and through continued commitment to service and practicing spiritual principles in all of my affairs, my spiritual awakening continued to expand exponentially.

In the wake of 9/11, the rooms of recovery in New York City were packed to the rafters with new members. In order to increase my ability to be of service in the rooms, I finally quit my job on Wall Street. From September 2001 until April 2002, I personally sponsored over two dozen men through the Steps, took on new service commitments at a number of meetings, began conducting "Back to Basics" Step seminars for groups while continuing to do service at ground zero, and posted up at St. Paul's Chapel in lower Broadway, delivering food to service workers.

After 9/11, I found it very difficult to sleep in my New York City apartment and would often break out in hives while walking around the Big Apple. It was suggested to me that I might have post-traumatic stress disorder (PTSD). That turned out to be true, and I began eye movement desensitization and reprocessing (EMDR) trauma therapy.

With the God of my understanding absolutely running the Gary show, our Creator had indeed entered into my heart and my life in a way that was truly miraculous. I wanted to take our relationship to the next level. I felt compelled to take a break from the din of Manhattan and find the quiet I needed to get clear about my calling and discern God's will for me.

On Easter Sunday, I checked into a monastery in Kentucky and attempted to take a vow of silence—which I didn't do very well. I scrubbed floors and meditated for many months, practicing Step Eleven and improving my conscious contact with the God of my "misunderstanding."

During this extended period of meditation and silent contemplation, it became clear to me that I was not meant to live exclusively in Step Eleven. Something was missing, and I knew what it was: I needed to carry the message of recovery. On several occasions, I snuck away from the monastery and hitchhiked to the nearest town in order to attend recovery meetings. I craved conversation with other drunks and addicts in recovery.

It was at the Abbey of Gethsemani that I rededicated my life to carrying the message of recovery to as many people as possible. I took off my cassock and returned to New York City.

I had been away from my recovery community at home for a long time, and attending meetings and reconnecting with my sponsees and friends in recovery was absolute bliss. I began attending at least six meetings every day and went to every sober event I could find. I couldn't get enough of it. Once again, I began receiving phone calls asking me to share my story of drinking, drugging, and recovery.

Now back in my old New York City studio, my morning and evening prayers included asking God to increase my territory for Twelve Step service and to show me new ways to carry the message of recovery in order to reach as many people as possible. At the same time, I began to have nightmares that involved a producer I had worked with off and on for nearly twenty years. A decade earlier, while still an active drunk and drug addict, I was portraying the role of Captain Hook in a national tour of *Peter Pan* and showed up for a performance three sheets to the wind. A heated argument began with this producer (who was also my boss) that escalated into ridiculous violence, and I was summarily and deservedly fired and tossed out of the theater. Before throwing me out of the stage door and into the back parking lot, he shouted, "This is show *business,* not show *friends!*" and slammed the door.

This producer was on my original Eighth Step list, and I had not yet made my amends. I had placed his name in the "later, maybe never, column" and contemplated this situation many times. I knew now that if I made the amends, the nightmares would stop. The hour was nigh, and I was willing.

But before making amends to this man, I wanted to be certain that I didn't have any ulterior motives and that I no longer needed show business in my life. I knew in the deepest part of my being that I didn't want there to be anything I needed from him in return for making my amends and wanted my motives to be pure. Late on a Sunday evening, I phoned my former theatrical boss. The next afternoon we met at a diner in Manhattan's theater district. I named out loud every harm I felt I had caused him and then spent time naming out loud all of the good that he had brought into my life. I then asked him to name any harms that I had forgotten. The experience was very emotional.

We spent the day together. As we were about to take our leave of one another, I extended my hand to shake his. Misty-eyed, he said "Gimme a hug, ya big bastard" and, while hugging me, he whispered, "Show *friends*." In that moment, we were both set free.

A few days later, I received a call from him. He told me that he had Googled the Twelve Steps, and he asked me if I was truly willing to go to any lengths to make my amends. He asked me to play the role of Sheriff Ed Earl in a national tour of *The Best Little Whorehouse in Texas,* followed by a tour of *Peter Pan.* I was flabbergasted. The combined tours would span a period of two years on the road.

Through working the Steps, turning over my will, and carrying the message, my past was no longer a liability. Everything had come full circle. God had restored my life and my mind to sanity.

I had a personal epiphany. The ministry I was seeking involved combining my passion for Step Twelve with the skills I had developed during my years as a performing artist, director, and producer. I saw my former profession in musical theater through new sober lenses. Through music, story, and laughter, the actor as priest tells a parable about the human condition, carrying a message of hope and love to the audience/congregation and uniting the gathered community—one mind, one body, one spirit—to provide healing. This was a radical shift in my perception. The Steps were becoming a part of my DNA. Looking for new ways to be of maximum service to God and my fellows had become a habit.

Word was out among my former friends in the theater business that I was sober and "trodding the boards" once again. I received a phone call from another producer offering me the role of Reverend Shaw in a revival of *Footloose*. The pay was several thousand per week.

That same day, I received a phone call from a director at a theater in South Florida whom I had never met. He had caught my performance in *The Best Little Whorehouse in Texas* during the national tour and he asked me to reprise my role of Sheriff Ed Earl in their production of that musical. The pay was a few hundred bucks a week and barely enough to cover my bills.

I asked both producers to give me a week to pray and marinate on it. Each day, I sat in silence asking for guidance: I was learning to listen to the still, small voice of God deep in my heart.

I chose "Door Number Two"—the theater in South Florida.

The day I arrived for my sober theatrical adventure, I was interviewed by a South Florida entertainment magazine. The interview was going to take fifteen to twenty minutes—just a short blurb in the publication—to promote our upcoming production of *The Best Little Whorehouse*.

At the top of the interview, I shared with the reporter that I was a recovering alcoholic and detailed my new way of thinking about my work as a theatrical artist. She turned off the tape recorder and shared with me that she had been in Al-Anon for over two decades. The interview lasted for several hours and turned into a two-page cover story that included some of my recovery story and my witness to the healing power of the Twelve Steps.

The day the article hit the newsstand, I received a phone call from one of the owners of the Florida theater I was now employed by. He had read the article and wanted to have lunch with me. He told me that he might be an alcoholic, and he wanted to talk with me about it.

In a flash, I knew why God had moved me to choose Florida. I grabbed my Big Book, the *Twelve Steps and Twelve Traditions*, and my copy of *Twenty-Four Hours a Day* and drove off to meet the man and get to work.

This was a Twelfth Step call, pure and simple. By the end of the afternoon, he was convinced that he and his wife were both alcoholics. I carried the message to him that there was a solution to their common problem, and I told him my story.

He said he was terrified to go to meetings—people might see him, and he wasn't ready for that. Then he tried to change the subject. He asked if I had ever heard of a play that had opened off Broadway called *Bill W. and Dr. Bob*—the story about the cofounders of AA, their wives, and how they met during the depths of the Great Depression. I had attended performances in New York City several times and had fallen in love with how this inspiring historic drama had been tailor-made for the stage.

Suddenly God gave me a divine idea. It was the dead of summer. My new friend's theater had a small black box performance space with nothing on the schedule. I suggested that we obtain the rights to the *Bill W. and Dr. Bob* play and mount a production. I assured him that every recovering drunk in Lee County, Florida, would come to see it. He was intrigued. I suggested that we codirect and coproduce a production, and then I handed him the Big Book and told him to read it so that he would understand the play. He agreed.

I cast myself in the role of Bill W., and we put out an audition notice for actors in recovery. We hired a cast composed of ten actors, all members from various Twelve Step fellowships. I brought in my friend from New York—the "Colonel," the actor who had saved my life many years earlier—to play the role of Dr. Bob.

My newly sober friend and producer white-knuckled his way through rehearsals. The cast of *Bill W. and Dr. Bob* became his first home group. The rehearsals were like attending Twelve Step meetings. We conducted business according to the Twelve Traditions. He stayed sober. His wife, also one of our producers, began to attend rehearsals and she got sober. They are both sober to this day.

Each night from the stage, as I portrayed the role of Bill W., I would witness healing miracles as we carried the message of recovery through the powerful medium of live theater, reaching alcoholics and addicts who might not be reached in any other way.

We sold out our eight-week run and reached thousands of people, receiving hundreds of emails and letters giving testimony to the power of receiving the message through our production.

The authors of *Bill W. and Dr. Bob,* Stephen Bergman and Janet Surrey, flew in from Boston. We began talking about creating a tour. Within weeks, my newly sober producing partners and I formed a production company called One Show at a Time and commenced to produce the national tour of the acclaimed off-Broadway play *Bill W. and Dr. Bob.* We toured the United States, and, with the support of Hazelden, we brought our production to San Antonio during the seventy-fifth international AA convention.

I fell in love with the early history of what I consider America's greatest gift to the world—Twelve Step recovery. I began spending significant time conducting research in Akron at the archives and at Stepping Stones, the home of Bill W. and his wife, Lois. I was on fire with a quest to learn everything I could about the early history of the Twelve Step movement.

During the convention, I was interviewed and filmed by Northern Light Productions during a performance in which I portrayed Bill W.; the footage was to be included in a documentary they were going to make on Twelve Step recovery titled *One Day at a Time— The History, Hope, and Healing of 12 Step Recovery.* The producers invited me to serve as director of project development for the production. The project expanded to become an international Twelve Step recovery education campaign, and the film was slated for worldwide broadcast through PBS and the BBC, with a potential audience of six hundred million.

Then God granted me another divine idea and I wrote a new play, *Pass It On . . . An Evening with Bill W. & Dr. Bob*—with only two characters, Bill and Bob—detailing how our program works.

Through the powerful medium of live theater, we could directly carry the Twelfth Step message and reach people who might not be reached any other way. The first national tour opened in 2011— staged as if audience members are in a recovery meeting in 1949 with Bill and Bob as the speakers, sharing their personal stories of drinking and recovery. The play dramatized key events in recovery history, such as their legendary drinking sprees and the night they met at the Seiberling Gatehouse in Akron, Ohio, in 1935. The second act was crafted to tell the history of the Big Book and how it was published, and to detail the spiritual principles of the Twelve Steps and how they work. Our new recovery education theater project was adopted by the National Council on Alcoholism and Drug Dependence, the oldest and largest recovery advocacy organization in the world. The council had been conceived in 1944 by Bill and Lois Wilson and founded by Marty Mann, AA's first woman to achieve long-term sobriety.

Inquiries to book the show came flooding in from coast to coast in the United States and Canada and resulted in five national tours. I began receiving hundreds of invitations to share my recovery story in cities all over America and Canada. I became a frequent guest on network television talk shows and national recovery radio programs to talk about Twelve Step recovery and how it works. Offers came in to conduct Twelve Step history seminars and Step workshops, and to carry the message at treatment centers, schools, law enforcement agencies, military bases, churches, recovery conventions, and retreats.

Prodigious Twelfth Step work has definitely kept me sober— who has time to drink? They say that God never gives us more than we can handle, so I suit up, show up, and do the work that my commitment to being a Step Twelve warrior demands.

Through living in Step Twelve, I have received the precious gift of continued sobriety. Through Step Twelve, I have learned to love God, myself, and the people in my life. As long as I continue to carry the message of hope, I will never again be alone.

PART II

A History of Step Twelve

. . . in which we learn of the first three Twelfth Step calls that launched AA and how the founders worked Step Twelve

4

The Origins of Step Twelve

Practical experience shows that nothing will so much insure immunity from drinking as intensive work with other alcoholics.

Alcoholics Anonymous, 4th edition, p. 89

TWELFTH STEP CALL NUMBER ONE: BILL W.

It all began with what we would come to know as a Twelfth Step call.

In the late fall of 1934, chronic inebriant Bill Wilson sat alone in his kitchen drowning himself in booze. His drinking party was interrupted by the telephone. The cheerful voice on the other end of the line was Bill's favorite drinking buddy and the hardest boozer he had ever known—Ebby Thatcher.

Ebby announced that he had been entirely sober for two whole months and was now living at the Calvary Episcopal Mission on West Twenty-Third Street in Manhattan, working with other drunks, and making restitution for harms caused. Bill was so shocked you could have hit him in the face with a wet mop and he wouldn't have felt it.

Ebby was on fire with his newfound sobriety. He said that he had heard that Bill was in trouble and was on his way to Brooklyn Heights to talk to Bill about his drinking problem.

Not so very long before, Ebby was a crackpot drunk, locked up for "alcoholic insanity—a menace to society." He had driven his car though the wall of some old lady's kitchen. When the police arrived, he stepped out of his car, tipped his hat, and said "Excuse me, Madame, I am awfully sorry about your kitchen but may I trouble you for a cup of coffee?"

Bill invited Ebby over, and as Bill sipped on bathtub gin and pineapple juice, Ebby shared his message of hope and how he had found relief from the dark halls of insanity and alcoholism. Ebby didn't lecture Bill about his drinking—he simply talked about how he had been able to overcome his own alcoholic drinking by embracing certain spiritual practices of the Oxford Group, a 1930s nondenominational Christian organization whose principles of absolute honesty, purity, unselfishness, and love were a precursor to the Twelve Steps. There he sat across the kitchen table from Bill, sober and with love in his eyes, telling Bill that he had experienced a vital spiritual awakening by completely surrendering to the guidance of God through two-way prayer. He regaled Bill with stories about how he was staying sober by living the principles of absolute love, purity, honesty, and unselfishness; taking a daily thorough self-examination; making amends; and making a sincere effort to give of his time in service to others, with no expectation of reward.

The message about a spiritual solution and a program of action had been carried—the seeds had been planted.

Later, Bill couldn't get the sight of sober Ebby out of his head. After a few weeks of restrained drinking, Bill sobered up enough to leave the house and caught the A train from Brooklyn to Manhattan, headed for Calvary Mission. He wanted what Ebby had. The instant Bill came up out of the subway, he walked straight into a bar.

By the time he finally reached Calvary Church, he was three sheets to the wind in a full-blown blackout, singing hymns at the top of his lungs. Altar call had just begun. Before Ebby could stop him, Bill stumbled to the front, got on his knees, and gave his life to God. Years later, as he recounted the story, Bill W. remarked that he couldn't recall that incident himself but was told by Ebby that his surrender speech was very moving.

He then fled the church and into the arms of a wicked five-day bender of incomprehensible demoralization.

On December 11, 1934, Bill stumbled into Charles B. Towns Hospital and was admitted under the care of Dr. William D. "Silky" Silkworth. Upon arrival, Bill was violent and had the DTs. He was fitted into a cozy canvas pajama top—the kind that ties in the back. His detoxification began with a regimen of cold tomatoes, corn syrup, and the barbiturate and belladonna puke-and-purge treatment. Bill was thirty-nine years old.

Lois wanted to have him committed for the rest of his life, but Bill had been given the gift of desperation: He was ready to really listen when Ebby visited Bill at Towns Hospital, essentially making another Twelfth Step call. He talked to Bill about prayer and suggested that he consider seeking guidance from God. Ebby then shepherded Bill through the Oxford Group's program of action, which would later become Steps Four through Eight.

Late that night, after taking a thorough self-examination and moral inventory with the help of Ebby, Bill slipped into a deep depression. From his pit of despair, he became willing to go to any lengths to stop drinking and surrendered absolutely, crying, "I'll do anything, anything at all! If there be a God, let Him show Himself!"

The AA conference-approved biography *Pass It On* quotes Bill as he describes his "white light" conversion and awakening, which occurred after taking certain spiritual steps.

> What happened next was electric. "Suddenly, my room blazed with an indescribably white light. I was seized with an ecstasy beyond description. Every joy I had known was pale by comparison. The light, the ecstasy—I was conscious of nothing else for a time.

"Then, seen in the mind's eye, there was a mountain. I stood upon its summit, where a great wind blew. A wind, not of air, but of spirit. In great, clean strength, it blew right through me. Then came the blazing thought, 'You are a free man.' I know not at all how long I remained in this state, but finally the light and the ecstasy subsided. I again saw the wall of my room. As I became more quiet, a great peace stole over me, and this was accompanied by a sensation difficult to describe. I became acutely conscious of a Presence which seemed like a veritable sea of living spirit. I lay on the shores of a new world." (*Pass It On* 1984, 121)

The following morning Ebby returned and handed Bill a copy of William James's book *The Varieties of Religious Experience.* He read it voraciously cover to cover and discovered the significance of his spiritual experience.

He then began writing letters of amends to everyone he could think of and was discharged on December 18, 1934. He was now a free man, and he never drank again. Ebby's Twelfth Step call, subsequent sponsorship, and willingness to walk Bill through a program of action that applied certain spiritual principles saved Bill's life.

Immediately upon leaving the hospital, Bill and Lois joined the Oxford Group and Bill began doing service, working with drunks and trying to sober up every alcoholic in New York City. He became obsessed. It was all he talked about, all he thought about. He would chase drunks from one end of the island to the other: He was on a personal crusade. Dr. Silkworth told Bill that his preaching and moralizing to the "rum hounds" was driving them all away and suggested that he should talk only about his own illness, his drinking, and the nature of his conversion experience.

After five months of exhausting work with other drunks, not one man had achieved sobriety; yet Lois pointed out that her husband's epic efforts to help other drunks was keeping Bill sober.

TWELFTH STEP CALL NUMBER TWO: DR. BOB

In the spring of 1935, Bill Wilson was asked to arrange for a hostile takeover of a tire manufacturing subsidiary company and needed to travel to Akron, Ohio. This trip was only going to take three days, and Dr. Silkworth felt that Bill was on solid ground and was safe to go.

At the first business meeting in Akron, the deal fell through. Bill's partners abandoned him and raced back to New York City. Bill found himself in the lobby of the Mayflower Hotel—alone, tired, angry, resentful, hungry, and nearly broke.

At one end of the lobby was a noisy cocktail lounge. He found himself being pulled toward the bar with a desperate desire to get hammered, drown his sorrows, and forget it all. But suddenly his mind was filled with thoughts about what he had learned through the Oxford Group, and right there, in the middle of that hotel lobby, he bowed his head and practiced two-way prayer, seeking the guidance of God. In a flash he knew that the antidote to drinking was talking to another drunk.

He walked to the pay phone and noticed a church directory on the wall next to it. A name jumped out at him—the Reverend Walter F. Tunks, pastor of Grace Episcopal Church. Bill was a wordsmith, and in Vermont when you take a walk in the woods you are taking a "tunk," so that was hunch enough for him.

For the next two hours, he paced back and forth in the hotel lobby trying to find the courage to pick up the telephone, call Reverend Tunks, and admit out loud that he is an alcoholic and ask for help from a total stranger.

Finally, Bill made the call and told Tunks that he had been sober five months and was about to fall off the wagon, and that if he did he would be a dead man; he then said that he had received guidance from God that he needed to find another drunk to talk to in order to remain sober. He also mentioned he had joined the Oxford Group.

Reverend Tunks listened and, being familiar with the Oxford Group, responded by giving Bill the names and phone numbers of ten members who might be able to lead Bill to another alcoholic.

For two more hours Bill pumped nickel after nickel into the pay phone. They were all either busy or not home, or they hung up on him.

Finally, with his last nickel, Bill rang up the last name on the list, a man named Norman Shepard. Norman was late to catch a train for a business meeting in Chicago and in a hurry. He was a heavy drinker, and while he resented the fact that Reverend Tunks had given his phone number to a stranger seeking a drunk to talk to, he agreed to give Bill one more number to call—a woman named Henrietta Seiberling, who had often lectured Norman about his drinking.

Henrietta had a reputation as a force of nature; she was a teetotaler, a supporter of the temperance movement, and very active in the Akron Oxford Group, where she had organized "an alcoholic squad" that attempted to sober up drunks. She also happened to be the divorced daughter-in-law of Frank Seiberling, whose tire company subsidiary Bill had tried to wage a hostile takeover of earlier that day.

Bill steeled up his nerve and made the call.

He told Henrietta Seiberling that he was a rum hound from New York City, sober five months, and that he had just said a prayer and knew that he could stay sober one more day if he could just find another drunk to talk to. Henrietta shouted, "Manna from Heaven! Mr. Wilson, I have been expecting you. I had a vision that you would come." She insisted that Bill hop in a taxi immediately and come to her home, the gatehouse of the Seiberling mansion.

Henrietta interviewed Bill for the next three hours to prove that he was in fact a drunk now sober—which was ironic, as he had been interviewed a hundred times where he was trying to prove that he was *not* a drunk.

After being convinced that Bill was right for the job, Henrietta told him she had just the man for him to talk to—the husband of her best friend, Anne Smith. Henrietta and Anne had been trying to help him get sober for years.

His name was Dr. Bob Smith—who later became affectionately known by AAs across the world as Dr. Bob.

Dr. Bob was a proctologist—a rectal surgeon—and a very sick alcoholic. There was a joke among the medical community in Akron that when you went to see Dr. Smith you were betting your ass!

Henrietta phoned Dr. Bob's wife and shouted the good news: "The miracle has happened—the sober drinking man I saw in my vision is here in my living room. Bring Bob over right away!"

Unfortunately Bob had passed all capability of listening to anyone—Dr. Bob was bagged. While Anne was on the phone with Henrietta, Dr. Bob had been dancing around the living room with a large potted plant singing "Happy Mother's Day" at the top of his lungs and had passed out under the dining room table. Anne agreed to bring Bob over the next night—which actually was Mother's Day—Sunday, May 12, 1935.

On the drive to Henrietta's, Dr. Bob asked his wife, "What sort of egg is this sober bird? He's got fifteen minutes—fifteen minutes and then we are going home."

At 5:00 p.m. sharp, the Smith's knocked on Henrietta's door. Bob looked at his wife and repeated "Fifteen minutes. Fifteen minutes tops."

After introductions they sat down for dinner, and Dr. Bob had the shakes so bad he couldn't hold his fork. His coffee cup flew out of his hand and smashed on the floor. He choked on his food. Everyone just stared in shocked silence until Bill spoke up and asked if Bob would like to skip the rest of dinner and join him for a smoke. Henrietta escorted them into her tiny mudroom where they could smoke and speak privately.

Bill then shared his story of drinking and recovery with Bob. He talked about his conversion experience and how working with other drunks and a spiritual solution had kept him sober. Dr. Bob later said that Bill was the first living human with whom he had ever talked who intelligently discussed his problem from actual experience. He came to realize that only another drunk could understand what he had been going through. Bill talked his language, so he listened to him and came to trust in what he had to say.

Then—for the first time in his life, Bill got quiet and asked Bob to tell his story.

Before dinner, Bill had wanted to drink and so did Bob. But after talking to one another, something remarkable happened: the craving for alcohol had lifted. Neither man wanted to drink—they just wanted to keep talking.

As a direct result of Bill W.'s Twelfth Step call to Dr. Bob—one drunk talking to another, carrying the message of hope and the spiritual solution to alcoholism—Bill W. and Dr. Bob had experienced the healing power of what was to become the Twelve Step program of recovery.

Six hours after the two men entered that tiny room, the Smith family and Bill Wilson piled into Bob's Pierce-Arrow, and Bill moved in with the Smiths.

For the next three weeks, Bill and Bob were inseparable and felt safe in their friendship and their determination to help keep one another sober.

They talked about the Bible, Oxford, philosophy, William James, Carl Jung, how to talk to their wives, how to talk to other drunks, fast cars (which used to be a hobby of Bob's), and fast women (which used to be a hobby of Bill's). They could have talked about anything and everything, because as long as they were together, neither man felt the need to drink. They both believed that they could go anywhere—even into a bar—so long as they had a clear, sober purpose for being there.

A few days later, Dr. Bob received an invitation to attend the American Medical Association convention in Atlantic City. He hadn't missed one in twenty-five years and wanted to go, but Anne said absolutely not. Bill argued that they needed to learn to live in the real world, so finally, Anne relented and Bob caught the train for the convention.

He started drinking the minute he boarded the train. He drank every drop of Scotch they had on the train and then bought several quarts on his way to the hotel. That was on Sunday. He got tight that night, stayed sober Monday until after dinner, then proceeded to get hammered again. He started drinking in the bar and then went back to his hotel room to finish the job. He woke up Tuesday, started drinking, and decided to head back home before he completely disgraced himself. He bought four more quarts of liquor on his way to the train depot and woke up at a friend's house near Akron.

By the time Bill and Anne managed to get Bob back home, he was about to go into a seizure that could have killed him. Anne wanted to send Bob to the sanitarium, but Bill begged Anne to allow him to continue working with Bob. He fed him cold tomatoes for vitamins and Karo corn syrup for energy, and then he administered whiskey and "goofballs"—the barbiturate sedatives that Bob had hidden away in his sock drawer—and put Dr. Bob to bed. Bob was scheduled to perform an operation three days later. The morning of the surgery, Bob announced that he was going to go through with it. His hands were still shaking so severely that Bill and Anne had to help him into his clothes. By the time they reached Akron City Hospital, he was twitching so badly that Bill was afraid his trembling scalpel was going to cut somebody a new one, but Dr. Bob assured everyone that he had surrendered his scalpel and his hands into the care of God.

Bill gave Bob one bottle of beer to steady his nerves and that beer, taken on June 10, 1935, was Dr. Bob's last drink.

The surgery went well. The patient survived and so did Bob.

After the operation, Dr. Bob drove all over Akron making amends to everyone he had ever harmed. He arrived home in the middle of the night, and in the presence of Anne and Bill W., he got on his knees and made his surrender to God.

The next day they immediately began looking for other drunks to try their new program on. Dr. Bob felt they needed to test their theories out on others to prove that it wasn't a fluke. So they tried it on their first "pigeon"—another doctor. Bill and Bob made a cold call to his home and talked to him about his drinking in front of his wife. The doctor was furious and threw them out of his home, feeling that he had been ambushed, and they learned their first lesson about how not to work with drunks—don't confront people in front of their loved ones without permission.

They began visiting saloons, attempting to carry the message, and learned another valuable lesson—never talk sobriety to a drunk while he's sitting in a bar.

They needed to find a third man who not only needed but also wanted what they had, and so, each morning, they would gather around the kitchen table and sit in silence asking for guidance.

Bill would always make the coffee, Bob would read from the Bible, and Anne would lead them in prayer. She would always finish her prayer by saying "faith without works is dead," and then she would jump up and give the men their marching orders: "I've got housework to do—you two go out and find yourselves a drunk to work on."

During morning meditation, they received guidance to carry their message to desperate men. Dr. Bob knew that there was a steady stream of sick boozers already in the hospital, men who had nothing left to lose and might be willing to listen. On June 26, 1935, Dr. Bob rang up Nurse Hilda Hall, and she told him that she had a fresh one who had tried to punch her in the eye and she had knocked him out. Hilda was a tough old bird, but she said she could use some help with this one.

TWELFTH STEP CALL NUMBER THREE: BILLY D.

So Dr. Bob and Bill Wilson drove over to Akron City Hospital to meet their man and get to work. Billy D. was a lawyer, former city councilman, and Sunday school teacher. There he was—thin as a rail, white as the bed sheets, bug-eyed, and terrified. He thought they were undertakers come to measure his body. Curled up in a ball, sweaty, unshaven, and stinking to high heaven—he had puked on the bed—Billy D. was a profound reminder of where they had been. Their hearts went out to him.

Bob spoke first: he told him how much he drank and for how long, and about the harm he had caused his wife and children. Bill then told him about his blackouts and binges, his financial shambles, legal troubles, the lies, jails, and sanitariums.

Billy D. never said one single word. He just sat there nodding.

Then they talked about their hiding places—water tank of the toilet, ash container of the furnace, dog house. Dr. Bob used to leave the house with a half dozen four-ounce bottles stuffed in his socks. One night he took his wife to the movies to see *Tugboat Annie* and found out that Wallace Beery used the same hiding place. Anne got down on the floor, right there in the movie theater, and pulled down his socks!

When Dr. Bob and Bill started to laugh, Billy D. laughed with them. His shoulders relaxed, his spirits seemed lighter, and so did theirs.

For a long while they just sat silently by his bedside, and finally Billy D. spoke up. He said he didn't think this thing would work for him, but he thought they were real nice fellas and if they were ever in the neighborhood again to be sure to visit him.

Bill told him that they would come back tomorrow, and the next afternoon when Bill W. and Dr. Bob walked into Billy D.'s hospital room, he took one look at them and he started screaming at the top of his lungs, "They's real! They's real! They's not spooks! They's real!" The nurses had to strap him down.

Poor old Billy D. had lain up in that hospital room all night unable to sleep, afraid he had lost his mind. He thought he had imagined Bill and Bob in an alcoholic hallucination. When he finally calmed down, he told them that he had never heard anyone speak so clearly about what he had been going through. He said he'd like to stick with them—he wanted what they had, and if they could do it, he could do it too.

Then Bob told him that he had to make a surrender to God, and if he didn't have a God he liked, he could borrow his—but they weren't leaving until he surrendered.

Around midnight, Dr. Bob finally got Billy on his knees.

Twelve Stepping often isn't easy. Bill W. said they probably could have had him on his knees earlier if Billy had talked faster. He was from the Deep South, and he talked so slow that Bill wanted to reach down his throat and pull the words out of his mouth.

They had found a third man who needed and wanted what they had. Now they were a "group."

Bob and Bill took their Twelfth Step call to the streets. They would scoop up a drunk and cart him off to the hospital, where he didn't even get a hospital gown, robe, or slippers and remained in the clothes that he came in. They were learning not to coddle them. If they puked on themselves, they'd leave them that way. If they wanted to sleep on the floor—so be it. They would just stand there and talk. They talked to men in beds sometimes for five or six hours until some of them couldn't stand it any longer and asked Bill and Bob to leave. They used all of the tools they had at the time—what they had learned about alcoholism through their personal experience, the Bible if the man was religious, and what they learned from the Oxford Group—but most of the time they just told their stories.

After dozens of failed attempts to find a fourth man who was willing to listen and try their new "program," they gradually began to find men who were ready to hear their message.

Always willing to go to any lengths to try to help a suffering alcoholic, Dr. Bob began to employ a secret weapon on some of his fresh drunks. It was a powerful sedative called paraldehyde. When a drunk would take a drink after the paraldehyde, he would be so sick he would often throw up his hands and say "All right, I've had enough! I'm not going to drink any more of that white stuff," and Bob and Bill knew he was ready to listen.

Bob would get to work on him first and send Bill in for the close. No matter how long it took, Dr. Bob always got them on their knees: making a surrender was a requirement.

Once a drunk would leave the hospital, they'd keep tabs on him. Most would still fail and go back to drinking, but every now and then one of their new pigeons saw the light, and those who did would join their little coffee club on Ardmore Street in Dr. Bob's front parlor. Together they learned a great deal about how to work with drunks and effectively carry the message and transmit their new spiritual recovery program of action. By the beginning of 1938, their little group had grown to forty recovered men in Akron.

THE FELLOWSHIP EXPANDS

At this point it was a word-of-mouth process only. Variations on their message were starting to spring up, and Bill wanted to solidify their program so it didn't get away from them. Also, due to a lack of standardized instruction, the growth of the fellowship was painfully slow. Bill W. admonished the small fellowship: "Within gunshot of this house, alcoholics are dying like flies. And if this thing doesn't move any faster than it has in the last three years it may be another ten before it gets to the outskirts of Akron."

Dr. Bob's granddaughter Penny Smith Umbertino shared with me that her father, Bob Jr., always said, "If it had been up to Dr. Bob, it would still be an eleven-bed operation in Akron; if it had been up to Bill, he would have franchised it and sold it in 1938." Thank God it wasn't up to Bill or Bob alone to ensure the continued existence and growth of our fellowship. It was up to the members themselves, acting out the will of a Power greater than self. As it was wisely inscribed in the Second Tradition, "For our group purpose there is but one ultimate authority—a loving God as He may express Himself in our group conscience. Our leaders are but trusted servants; they do not govern."

By the end of 1938, one hundred men had recovered in Akron, New York City, and Cleveland.

Bill W. felt the urgent need to create some sort of written manifesto or textbook, to clearly define and memorialize a simple and consistent set of spiritual principles and a program of recovery that would reach more drunks with this lifesaving message.

Alcoholics Anonymous, or as it later came to be called, the Big Book, was written with input from several of the founding members and published in April 1939. In October of that same year, a series of articles about AA appeared in the *Cleveland Plain Dealer,* resulting in rapid growth of the fellowship in Northeast Ohio, and by the end of 1939, four hundred had recovered.

Sales of the Big Book were slow at first, but in April 1941, the AA program and way of life were featured as the cover story by Jack Alexander for the *Saturday Evening Post*—the most widely circulated magazine in America—and virtually overnight, seven thousand copies of the Big Book sold.

People everywhere were rushing out to bookstores to purchase a copy of the Big Book, and meetings began popping up like wildflowers from coast to coast—in Toledo, Kalamazoo, Los Angeles, Little Rock, Detroit—and by the end of 1941, more than eight thousand people had recovered.

Beginners meetings were developed that enabled newcomers to be taken through the Steps quickly—saving their lives and creating a new army of sponsors who were willing and able to pass it on. Working all Twelve Steps and then passing it on to others was a requirement for membership.

> It was soon evident that a scheme of personal sponsorship would have to be devised for the new people. Each prospect was assigned an older A.A., who visited him at his home or in the hospital, instructed him on A.A. principles, and conducted him to his first meeting. But in the face of many hundreds of pleas for help, the supply of elders could not possibly match the demand. Brand-new A.A.'s, sober only a month or even a week, had to sponsor alcoholics still drying up in the hospitals. (*Alcoholics Anonymous Comes of Age* 1985, 20–21)

It had all begun with what we now know as a Twelfth Step call, when Ebby Thatcher carried a message of hope to Bill W.—which was the same message Bill carried to Dr. Bob. Through painful trial and error, and from hard-won personal experience, our founders knew that working with others and carrying the message was the vital and essential heart of our program.

When their groundbreaking new program of Twelve Step recovery was finally standardized in the Big Book, a full chapter, chapter 7, was devoted entirely to Step Twelve and chapters 8, 9, and 10 were devoted to how to carry the message and work with others. No other Step is given such importance as Step Twelve.

Having had a spiritual awakening as a result of practicing the principles of love and service in all of their affairs, our founders were able to transmit the healing miracle of recovery to over one hundred thousand men and women by the close of 1950. Due to rigorous Twelfth Step work, the membership continued to double every year until the 1990s.

As a direct result of individual members living in Step Twelve and carrying the message to those who still suffer, this magnificent cathedral of the spirit has reached around the globe to 170 nations; has expanded into Al-Anon and dozens of other Twelve Step programs that offer hope, transformation, and healing for a host of human problems; and has become one of America's greatest gifts to the world.

Whenever anyone anywhere reaches out for help, the hand of Twelve Step recovery must always be there—and for that we are responsible.

Without Twelfth Step work, we would cease to exist. Our future is in our hands.

5

The Golden Age of Twelve Steppers—How the Founders Worked Step Twelve

⚜

Within six years after Bill W. Twelfth Stepped Dr. Bob at the Gatehouse in Akron, it is estimated that as many as eight thousand men and women had recovered from the seemingly hopeless state of mind, body, and spirit that characterizes the disease of alcoholism. For the first time since humans crushed grapes to make wine, the spiritual program of Alcoholics Anonymous had provided a dependable solution to the problem of alcoholism.

This disease had become an epidemic in America in the 1930s, and the early Twelve Step pioneers were on fire with a passion to carry their message to a sick and suffering world plagued with untreated alcoholism. They understood beyond a shadow of a doubt that in order to maintain their sobriety and ensure the continued existence of our program and our way of life, it was each and every member's spiritual duty to give back what was so freely given to them: the gift of sobriety. They were compelled to work intensively with others.

As a direct result of prodigious and rigorous Twelfth Step work, between 1941 and 1950—called by some the "golden age" of AA— the fellowship mushroomed from six thousand to one hundred thousand members (Alcoholics Anonymous 2016) and groups reported recovery rates of 75 percent. (Henry 1997 and Dick B. 2006) Records in Cleveland and Akron in the 1940s show that 93 percent of their members never drank again—rates of success that have never been matched since. (*Dr. Bob and the Good Oldtimers* 1980, 261) Accurate statistics reflecting the current success rates of Twelve Step programs are nearly impossible to ascertain, though it is widely believed that in recent times the growth of our membership and our program's recovery success rate has declined precipitously. Not coincidentally, in recent times, many aspects of how our program is "worked" have been changed dramatically from the robust manner in which our forbearers applied the tools of our program during the golden age of AA.

The manner in which our founders worked Step Twelve brought about continued rapid growth of our membership, ensured quality long-term recovery for all, and saved lives in record numbers. How many of us today actually take the time to conduct Twelfth Step calls, become a sponsor, shepherd newcomers through all Twelve Steps, and give back what was so freely given to us? I invite you to ask for a show of hands at the next Twelve Step meeting you attend.

In our complex 21st century world, Twelve Step programs continue to work miracles for those who truly want to recover and are willing to go to any lengths to "work it." And yet, it is imperative that we ask ourselves "what were the recovery pioneers doing in in the 1940s in Akron and Cleveland that enabled them to achieve such consistent and astonishingly high rates of growth and lasting recovery?"

I believe that the secret of their success is found in the manner in which they thoroughly worked Step Twelve. Their work always included a fierce commitment to giving of themselves in service to others, conducting prolific Twelve Step calls, and a dedication to strong sponsorship. This mandated walking all new members through all Twelve Steps quickly and as often as needed to relieve their suffering and help them to build a strong bulwark of defense against picking up a drink. For every member, becoming a sponsor was a foregone conclusion and an essential part of living in Step Twelve.

Typically, within the first thirty days of sobriety, a newcomer had reached Step Twelve and had begun the process of rewiring his brain, resulting in the profound spiritual awakening promised in that Step. This in turn empowered a new member to become a sponsor, and driven by a newfound passion for helping others, he would be compelled to quickly shepherd other suffering alcoholics through the Steps—extending the legacy of the Twelfth Step call.

During the early days, AA wasn't so easy to find. There was no intergroup office or published telephone number. Some AA members circulated their personal phone numbers privately among a group of sympathetic doctors, clergy, judges, and police officers. Besides the former drinking chums of sober AA members, new prospects were typically routed out while these members conducted their Twelve Step work in drunk tanks and the detox wards of local hospitals. They would go out in pairs, just as Bill and Dr. Bob had done with Billy D. They would share their stories of drinking and recovery, structuring their talk to follow a procedure known as "the five Cs," borrowed from the Oxford Group: Confidence, Confession, Conviction, Conversion, and Continuance.

> Confidence involves the establishment of rapport [between] the "life changer" and the person to be changed. Confession involves the admission of faults overcome by the "changed" individual for the purpose of encouraging the prospect. Conviction is the mental process by which the prospect becomes aware of his or her faults. Conversion is the change itself, based on a commitment to follow God's guidance. Not even a prior belief in God is ... necessary. To act as if there were a God is sufficient; a genuine belief in God frequently follows. Continuance ... strengthens and confirms conversion by seeking and following "guidance," and "changing" others. (Clark 1951, 28, edited for clarity)

These principles and techniques were later distilled and modified by Bill W. and incorporated into the Big Book.

During his tour of duty in France during World War I, Bill Wilson was in charge of raising carrier pigeons, which were used to carry messages to the front lines. He told Dr. Bob they needed to devise a system for quickly training a flock of new "pigeons"—what newcomers later came to be called—to go out and carry the message of Alcoholics Anonymous in order to maximize AA's ability to save lives and ensure the continued growth of our fellowship.

Cleveland AA member Clarence S. took up Bill's call to action and made a decision to work his Twelfth Step by giving out his telephone number to the front desk operator at the *Cleveland Plain Dealer.* His wife, Dorothy, who wasn't an alcoholic, unofficially became the first AA hotline operator, fielding the tsunami of incoming calls for help. When a call came in from a fresh prospect reaching out for help, Dorothy referred the call to Clarence at his place of business, an automobile dealership. His sales force were mostly fellow sober AAs, and Clarence would dispatch two of his best salesman to make a Twelfth Step call to "sell" the desperate on the AA program. These tireless pioneers sponsored newcomers as fast as humanly possible—one man at a time.

In 1941, when Jack Alexander's cover story featuring AA appeared in the *Saturday Evening Post,* the hinges blew off the door. The phones rang night and day. How could they meet the rising tide of need and demand for their revolutionary new program?

The first "central office" of AA was opened in Cleveland, and they published their phone number. Then Clarence S. was given a divine idea during his morning guidance. He formed a beginners meeting group with a format designed to introduce newcomers to the AA program and take them quickly and efficiently in four one- to two-hour sessions through the Twelve Steps in groups. The newcomer had to agree to attend all four beginners meetings on four consecutive Fridays with his sponsor, during which time they would complete all Twelve Steps. These meetings always opened with a speaker followed by a coffee break. Then the sponsor and his new pigeon would retire to a back room, where they were joined by other sponsors and their pigeons, and the Step Work would begin in earnest. They followed the prescription in the first edition of the Big Book, where the words used to describe taking Steps One through Nine—"next," "at once," "immediately," and "we waste no time"—were taken seriously. They used early AAs—beginning with Bill W. and continuing with Dr. Bob, Billy D., Earl T., and others—as role models to work all the Steps in days and weeks, not months.

DR. BOB'S "KEEP IT SIMPLE" APPROACH

AA pioneer Earl T. got sober in 1937 during a weekend trip to Akron. Dr. Bob sponsored Earl through the Steps in a few hours. Earl returned home to Chicago and began sponsoring other men and remained sober until his death. He recounts his experience of being sponsored by Dr. Bob:

> [On] Dr. Bob's afternoon off, he had me to the office and we spent three or four hours formally going through the Six-Step program as it was at that time. (*At the time it was a six-step program based on the Oxford Group's approach.*) The six steps were:
>
> 1. Complete deflation
> 2. Dependence and guidance from a Higher Power
> 3. Moral inventory
> 4. Confession
> 5. Restitution
> 6. Continued work with other alcoholics
>
> Dr. Bob led me through all of these steps. At the moral inventory, he brought up several of my bad personality traits such as selfishness, conceit, jealousy, carelessness, intolerance, ill-temper, sarcasm, and resentments. We went over these at great length and then he finally asked me if I wanted these defects of

character removed. When I said yes, we both knelt at his desk and prayed, each of us asking to have these defects taken away.

This picture is still vivid. If I live to be a hundred, it will always stand out in my mind. It was very impressive and I wish that every A.A. could have the benefit of this type of sponsorship today. (*Alcoholics Anonymous* 2001, 263)

Some of Dr. Bob's sponsees are alive as of this writing, with over fifty years of sobriety, and testify that they took the Steps either in the hospital or at Dr. Bob's office, just like Earl T. did. Dr. Bob was the prince of Twelve Steppers—from the day he took his last drink in 1935 until his death in 1950, he carried the message, sponsored, and taught the Steps to well over five thousand alcoholics.

Dr. Bob explains his "keep it simple" approach: "The Twelve Steps are simple and can be taken by anyone who wants to stop drinking. They are actions not theories or spiritual philosophies. They are not meant to be understood first then taken. They are survival actions that bring about immediate relief and hope, and are the tools by which a newcomer can draw on at any time to stay sober!"

The pioneers repeated some version of this simple and straightforward process thousands of times during the early days, with remarkable success. Imagine this scenario:

• • •

It's late Fall 1941. You live in Cleveland, Ohio. You are a sick alcoholic on death's doorstep—you have hit rock bottom. You learn about AA through a newspaper article in the Cleveland Plain Dealer. *You call AA and beg for help. You tell them that if you drink again you will die. The AAs believe you. They waste no time, and two members come to your aid at once. They know that you are passing through a slim window of opportunity when you are most teachable. These "Step Twelve Missionaries" tell you their stories to gain your confidence. They talk your language. You come to trust what they have to say. They share with you the good news that they have recovered as the result of a spiritual solution found by following a few simple steps. These two AAs together become your sponsors. (Everyone had two sponsors—even the cofounders Bill W. and Dr. Bob.)*

These Twelfth Step warriors transport you to a detox where you will dry out for the next three to five days. Your sponsors' home group regularly passed a basket to collect donations so that the group could help defray the costs of detox, so they pay your detox bill.

The next day, they come to visit you in the drunk ward. You are just coming to and are disoriented. You look at these two fresh-faced, sober men—they seem vaguely familiar. You mutter, "Where the hell am I? And who the hell are you?"

They chuckle—they've been where you are at. They know firsthand what it feels like when your brain is drying out and the fog is lifting.

For the next few days that you are in detox, these new friends bring with them other sober men from AA to share their stories. Being alcoholics themselves, they understand that alcoholics are tortured by loneliness and that you are in desperate need of making good human connections.

You are in great pain. They tell you that you have been given the gift of desperation. You have no idea what they are talking about, but you want what they have so you just nod and listen.

They tell you that if they can do it you can do it and that this AA thing really works.

Before you are discharged from the hospital, they take you through Steps One, Two, and Three, right then and there. At the end of the day, before they take their leave, you are told to get on your knees. You are required to make a surrender to God. They tell you that if you don't have a God you like, you can borrow theirs, but they are not leaving until you hit your knees. They assure you this AA thing has nothing to do with religion. It's just drunks helping one another find a spiritual solution to their common problem.

They ask if you are in need of a suit—you will need a decent suit to be able to find employment and to look presentable when you begin to make Twelfth Step calls after you complete your Steps and sponsorship training. You haven't got a good suit, so your new sober friends obtain one for you.

They now have a financial investment in your sobriety. They tell you that they need you to follow the AA rules and stay sober so that you can repay your debt during your Ninth Step amends. You have no idea what they are talking about and can't imagine ever being able to hold a job, much less pay them back.

Again they chuckle. They tell you not to worry—amends is part of working the Twelve Steps—and that more will be revealed to you when you attend your first AA meeting.

Upon your discharge from detox, they are there to greet you.

They buy you groceries and visit with you every day until Friday evening, when they both show up at your house in their car and take you to your first beginners Step meeting.

You meet dozens of other sober alcoholics and are made to feel welcome. Coffee is brewing. The air is blue with cigarette smoke. It looks like a political convention. Everyone looks so goddamn happy. Their joy annoys you.

You sit in the front row with your sponsors and listen to a speaker share his own story of drinking and recovery. The speaker shares with complete honesty about what he has been through—he speaks about tragic events in his life with complete freedom from embarrassment or remorse. The room is filled with laughter. You find yourself laughing also. You never thought you would laugh again. Tears are streaming down your face. You suddenly feel like you have come home.

After the speaker, your sponsors take you into a back room where you are led through the Fourth and Fifth Steps in one session. You are told that you will complete all Twelve Steps during the next couple of Fridays.

After the meeting, you are taken out for more coffee and doughnuts, and you talk about the Steps with your new friends until the wee hours.

These two men continue to shadow you for the next thirty days until your initial Step work has been completed.

Having completed the first eleven Steps, you become a sponsor in training. For a period of sixty days, you shadow your sponsors as they continue to conduct new Twelfth Step calls. You learn how to talk to drunks and their families.

Ninety days into your new sober life, you have completed your Steps, have been trained in how to conduct a Twelfth Step call, and are now qualified to become a sponsor, take newcomers through the Steps, and train your own pigeons to carry the message.

• • •

In those early days of AA, sponsorship put the responsibility for doing the work on the sponsor rather than on the sponsored. Those early AA members understood that without dedicated and diligent work with others, there could be no long-term recovery for anyone.

The need for this manner of rigorous, time-consuming, and often arduous Twelfth Step work was essential and critical—without this component, recovery would be tenuous at best and many would relapse and die.

In 1940, the Akron Group No. 1, with the help and encouragement of Dr. Bob, wrote a pamphlet for newcomers and sponsors designed to offer a practical explanation of what to do and what not to do as you sally forth as a sponsor on a Step Twelve mission. The pamphlet details what a sponsor's duties are in regard to helping your sponsee (often referred to as "babies" in those days) and how you should conduct yourself while visiting patients—as the vast majority of members found their way to those early AA groups from hospitals and institutions. The pamphlet also helped newcomers learn what to do in their search for sobriety.

This pamphlet was written and distributed within one year of the publication of the Big Book and was to be read in conjunction with the AA basic text as a part of Dr. Bob's sponsorship training program.

I close this chapter with some excerpts from Dr. Bob's home group pamphlet to give you an idea of the extent of commitment that early members made to working Step Twelve, with hopes that it will awaken a similar commitment in you to bring this Step alive in your program of recovery. The program has changed dramatically since those early days, and we will be exploring in the remaining chapters how we can apply these same principles in developing our own Twelfth Step practice.

It is desirable that each member of A. A. furnish each of his prospective members with this "Manual" when he first calls on him, particularly in the case of hospitalization.

The experience behind the writing and editing of this pamphlet adds up to hundreds of years of drinking plus scores of years of recent sobriety. Every suggestion is backed up by hard experience.

The editors do not pretend any explanation of the spiritual or religious aspects of A. A. It is assumed that this phase of the work will be explained by sponsors.

Definition of an Alcoholic Anonymous:

An Alcoholic Anonymous is an alcoholic who, through application of and adherence to rules laid down by the organization, has *completely* foresworn the use of any and all alcoholic beverages. The moment he wittingly drinks so much as a drop of beer, wine, spirits, or any other alcoholic beverage he automatically loses all status as a member of Alcoholics Anonymous.

A. A. is not interested in sobering up drunks who are not sincere in their desire to remain completely sober for all time. It is not interested in alcoholics who want to sober up merely to go on another bender; sober up because of fear for their job, their wife, or to clear up some trouble, either real or imaginary. In other words, if a person is genuinely sincere in his desire for continued sobriety for his own good, is convinced in his own heart that alcohol has got him down, and is willing to admit that he is an alcoholic, Alcoholics Anonymous will do all in their power, spend days of their time to guide him to a new, a happy way of life.

It is utterly essential for the newcomer to sincerely say to himself, "I am doing this for myself and myself alone." Experience has proved in hundreds of cases that unless an alcoholic is sobering up for a purely personal and selfish motive, he will not last. He may remain sober for a few weeks or a few months, but the moment the motivating element, generally fear of some sort, disappears, so disappears sobriety.

To the ladies: If we seem to slight you in this booklet it is not intentional. We merely use the masculine pronouns "he" and "him" for convenience. We fully realize that alcohol shows no partiality. It does not respect age, sex, nor estate. The millionaire drunk on [the best] Scotch looks just like the laboring man drunk on [the cheapest] wine when he is lying in the gutter or the hospital bed. . . . Every word in this pamphlet applies to women as well as men.

A word to the sponsor who is putting his first newcomer into a hospital or otherwise introducing him to this new way of life: You must assume full responsibility for this man. He trusts you, otherwise he would not submit to hospitalization. You must fulfill all pledges that you make to him, be they tangible or intangible. If you cannot fulfill a promise do not make it. It is easy to promise a man that he will get his job back if he will sober up. But unless you are certain that it can be fulfilled, don't make that promise. Don't promise financial aid unless you are ready to keep your part of the bargain. If you don't know how he is going to pay his hospital bill, don't put him in the hospital unless you are willing to assume financial responsibility.

It is definitely your job to see that he has visitors and you must visit him frequently yourself. If you put a man in a hospital and then neglect him, he will naturally lose confidence in you, assume a "nobody loves me" attitude, and your half-hearted labors will be lost.

Don't coerce him into a hospital. Don't get him drunk and then throw him in while he is unconscious. Chances are that when he sobers up he won't last.

You should be able to judge if a man is sincere in his desire to quit drinking. Use this judgment. Otherwise, you will find yourself needlessly bumping your head into a stone wall and wondering why your "babies" don't stay sober. Remember your own experience. You can remember many a time when you would have done anything to get over that awful alcoholic sickness, although you had no desire in the world to give up alcohol for good. It doesn't take much good health to inspire an alcoholic to go back and do the things over again that made him sick.

You should see that your patient has the proper literature, such as "Alcoholics Anonymous," this pamphlet, the "Upper Room," a Bible if possible, and any other literature that has helped you. Impress upon him the wisdom and necessity of reading and rereading this literature.

Study the newcomer and decide who, among your A. A. friends, might have the best story and exert the best influence on him. There are all types in A. A. and regardless of whom you hospitalize there are dozens whose stories will help him. An hour on the telephone will produce callers. Don't depend on chance. Stray visitors will drop in, but twenty or thirty phone calls will clinch matters and remove uncertainty. It is your responsibility to conjure up callers.

When your patient is out of the hospital your work has not ended. It is now your duty not only to him but to yourself to see that he starts out on the right foot. See to it that he gets to his first meeting and accompany him on his first hospital call. Telephone him when you know of other patients.

Remember, you depend on the newcomer's sobriety to keep you sober as much as he depends on you!

Never lose touch with your responsibility. Drop into his home or his office occasionally. Telephone him. Talk to him at meetings. Encourage him to look you up.

Your responsibility never ends. (excerpt from *A Manual for Alcoholics Anonymous* 1940, 1–5)

PART III

Working Step Twelve Today

❦

*. . . in which we learn to apply Step Twelve in all our affairs,
including the vital role of sponsorship and making a life
of service relevant in the twenty-first century*

6

The Art of the Twelfth Step Call

Having had a spiritual awakening as the result of working Steps One through Eleven, I am now compelled from the depths of my very soul to freely give to others the love that has been given to me by offering the healing spiritual solution of the Twelve Steps to those who are still sick and suffering.

Step Twelve is the spiritual centerpiece of our program, the heart of which is the Twelfth Step call and working with others. In the Big Book, on page 89 we learn:

> Practical experience shows that nothing will so much insure immunity from drinking as intensive work with other alcoholics. It works when other activities fail. This is our *twelfth suggestion:* Carry this message to other alcoholics! You can help when no one else can. You can secure their confidence when others fail.

In order to comprehensively practice the Twelfth Step, we must embrace an ongoing commitment to conduct Twelfth Step calls, shepherd others through the Twelve Steps, and share our experience, strength, and hope wherever and whenever our Higher Power crosses our paths with anyone who suffers from our common malady of mind, body, and spirit. In the words of Bill W., "We must never be so anonymous that it prevents us from helping someone."

Many find Step Twelve to be the most challenging of the Steps. It demands that we literally step out of our comfort zone, transcend our fears and feelings of self-doubt, and give our time and resources generously and freely in the service of others. My story demonstrates how, as a direct result of giving of myself through Twelfth Step service work, I have been given a life beyond my wildest dreams.

When we give ourselves completely in service to others:

> Life will take on new meaning. To watch people recover, to see them help others, to watch loneliness vanish, to see a fellowship grow up about you, to have a host of friends—this is an experience you must not miss. (*Alcoholics Anonymous* 2001, 89)

Twelfth Step work is simple, but it isn't always easy. If it were easy, everyone would do it all of the time. Cultivating this spirit of service requires practice and discipline. Maintaining our spiritual condition often requires placing the welfare of others ahead of our own wants and needs.

In early sobriety, I was told that I had to be willing to go to any lengths to get what Twelve Step recovery had to offer. Now that I have been given the gift of some years of continuous sobriety, one day at a time, I must continue to be willing to go to any lengths to keep what this program has given me.

Once we have completed and are practicing the first eleven Steps, we learn that we are ready to carry out our marching orders as a Step Twelve soldier in the army of light.

> Your job now is to be at the place where you may be of maximum helpfulness to others, so never hesitate to go anywhere if you can be helpful. You should not hesitate to visit the most sordid spot on earth on such an errand. Keep on the firing line of life with these motives and God will keep you unharmed. (*Alcoholics Anonymous* 2001, 102)

It is through intensive work with others that recovery from this disease truly becomes my greatest asset as I take on the role of the wounded healer. It is through Twelfth Step service that we become miracle workers and develop an intimate working relationship with our Higher Power. There is no question in my mind that I wouldn't have stayed clean and sober all of these years without my willingness to embrace this action step and conduct prodigious Twelfth Step calls and sponsor others through their Step work. Each time I make a Twelfth Step call and work with others, I gain new insights in our lifesaving program. Twelfth Step service work keeps the solution front and center in my brain and my heart.

It's important to keep in mind that *we will never be able to lay claim to having completed Step Twelve.* This Step is a Higher-Powered ongoing action Step, where we endeavor to incorporate service work into every aspect of our lives. As members of a Twelve Step community, our primary purpose is to help others become healthy and spiritually fit. Practicing Step Twelve in all of our affairs makes that possible.

Practically every time I share my story, someone will approach me wanting help. They often start out by saying "I don't want to bother you—but could I get your phone number? I need a sponsor." I tell them that this recovery deal isn't just about you—it's also about me. You don't get sober alone, and I don't stay sober alone. We do this thing together. I must give away what I have in order to keep what I have been given. Each time we conduct a Twelfth Step call and start someone on their pathway through the Steps, we gain a deeper understanding about this lifesaving spiritual program and receive new inspiration and insights that will sustain our ongoing recovery.

GETTING STARTED

Many of us are hesitant to make Twelfth Step calls. We fear that we are not adequately prepared to take on this challenge, which at first glance appears to be too daunting. We think that we are to assume responsibility for getting the newcomer sober, and we fear that we won't be successful. But always remember this: the purpose of a Twelfth Step call is to keep us sober—that is the measure of its success. We aren't responsible for how other people respond to our story and how well we present the Steps. Some get it and some don't. We take no credit for the ones who get it, and we do not become remorseful over the ones who don't. We move on to the next opportunity to be helpful, knowing that there are legions of sick alcoholics and addicts who are dying to get what we have. Some are already in treatment programs, jails, and prisons in our community and present a ready audience for you and your Twelve Step group to tell your stories to (more about this later). Others are individuals in your community who are at various stages of awareness about their alcohol and other drug use, and its effect on their lives and those around them.

We may hear about these people from family members, friends, work associates, on Facebook, or even in casual conversation at a social gathering. Most often they will come into the rooms having been sent there by a spouse, parent, clergy person, or a doctor, usually after multiple crises that have arisen due to their drinking or other drug use. Many come out of treatment programs at various stages of readiness to fully commit to recovery.

There are many ways to come in contact with people who need your help. Become a greeter at meetings or serve the coffee or refreshments, and when you see an unfamiliar face, ask "are you new to the rooms or are you just new to me?" You can also answer the phones at your local intergroup and sign up for Twelfth Step call duty through your local General Service Office.

When you've identified someone who needs help, it's important to stay focused on your role in making a Twelfth Step call, which is to help people see that alcohol or other drugs have had a negative impact on their lives, that they may be an alcoholic or addict, that addiction is a disease, and that the spiritual solution found through a Twelve Step program can help them recover from that disease. With that understanding, your primary responsibility then is to get them to a Twelve Step meeting if they aren't attending one already and continue supporting them in working the Steps. When possible, it's advisable to make a Twelfth Step call in pairs, just as the early AA members did, especially when you're starting out.

People whose addiction is severe enough will probably need to go into detox and possibly an inpatient program, especially if they have a co-occurring psychological disorder, such as depression or PTSD, or underlying physical health issues. Others may be able to use one of the many outpatient programs, which will allow them to continue to work or go to school.

It is also helpful to understand some of the criteria for addiction in order to determine the kind of help your prospects may need. Not everyone who abuses alcohol or drugs is an addict, and some who are addicts may be able to stop or cut down on their own without Twelve Step recovery. It's not your job to diagnose them or determine the severity of their addiction and treatment needs—there are professionals for that.

The questions we ask during a Twelfth Step call regarding our prospects' drinking and drugging habits and experiences are to determine if our prospects believe they are alcoholic and if they have come to a point where they are ready to go to any lengths to recover.

In the *Manual for Alcoholics Anonymous,* written in 1940 by Dr. Bob's home group, they offer a list of questions to ask our prospects. The answers to these questions may become the basis of our new friend's First Step, which we will take them through during our first visit.

> The prospective member of A.A. may have some doubts if he is actually an alcoholic. A.A. in Akron has found a yardstick prepared by psychiatrists of Johns Hopkins University to be very valuable in helping the alcoholic decide for himself.
>
> Have your prospect answer the following questions, being as honest as possible with himself in deciding the answers. If he answers YES to one of the questions, there is a definite warning that he MAY be an alcoholic. If he answers YES to any two, the

chances are that he IS an alcoholic. If he answers YES to any three or more, he IS DEFINITELY an alcoholic and in need of our help.

The questions:

1. Do you lose time from work due to drinking?
2. Is drinking making your home life unhappy?
3. Do you drink because you are shy with other people?
4. Is drinking affecting your reputation?
5. Have you gotten into financial difficulties as a result of drinking?
6. Have you ever stolen, pawned property, or "borrowed" to get money for alcoholic beverages?
7. Do you turn to lower companions and an inferior environment when drinking?
8. Does your drinking make you careless of your family's welfare?
9. Has your ambition decreased since drinking?
10. Do you crave a drink at a definite time daily?
11. Do you want a drink the next morning?
12. Does drinking cause you to have difficulty in sleeping?
13. Has your efficiency decreased since drinking?
14. Is drinking jeopardizing your job or business?
15. Do you drink to escape from worries or troubles?
16. Do you drink alone?
17. Have you ever had a complete loss of memory as a result of drinking?
18. Has your physician ever treated you for drinking?
19. Do you drink to build up your self-confidence?
20. Have you ever been to a hospital or institution on account of drinking?

Asking your prospects these twenty questions will help them reach clarity for themselves as to whether or not they are powerless—the first step on the road to transformation and healing.

Our Twelfth Step calls will often include taking our new friends through the first three Steps. In the beginning of their recovery, the practical outcome of taking these first three Steps may mean being willing to work the rest of the Steps and turning their lives over to the care of their recovery group, or simply to G̲ood O̲rderly D̲irection.

The Big Book is a textbook and our training manual for this process and gives us a blueprint for working with others so that we can pass on what we have learned about working these Steps ourselves. This means that we have studied it and have begun to apply in our own recovery the principles and practices in the first 103 pages. Those pages describe the disease of alcoholism (in "The Doctor's Opinion" and chapters 1 through 4) and give us the program of action to recover from this disease (in chapters 5 through 7). In preparation for our first Twelfth Step call, we pay special attention to chapter 7, "Working with Others." In this chapter, we will find clear instructions detailing the most effective method through which we can transmit our lifesaving message of recovery to those who are still suffering—a proven and beta-tested method that enables us to bring our new friend to an understanding of our way of life.

Through developing our skills for the art of the Twelfth Step call, we are able to make deep and lasting human connections with alcoholics and addicts who still suffer. We offer them hope as we introduce them to our Twelve Step way of life and lay before them our spiritual tool kit designed to remove the blocks that separate them from the Great Power that will free them from the hell that they are living in and keep them sober for the rest of their lives, one day at a time.

Making a classic Twelfth Step call is actually pretty simple and straightforward. The Big Book gives us this basic instruction:

> When you discover a prospect for Alcoholics Anonymous, find out all that you can about him. If he does not want to stop drinking, don't waste time trying to persuade him. You may spoil a

later opportunity. . . . Get an idea of his behavior, his problems, his background, the seriousness of his condition, and his religious leanings. You need this information to put yourself in his place, to see how you would like him to approach you if the tables were turned. (*Alcoholics Anonymous* 2001, 90)

Much time and effort can be saved by learning the answers to these questions as soon as possible:

1. Do they really have a drinking problem?
2. Do they know they have a problem?
3. Do they want to do something about their drinking?
4. Do they want help?

Again, we don't try to diagnose people as an alcoholic or addict—we let them draw their own conclusions. We never moralize or present ourselves as better than they are because we are them—the only difference being that by the grace of our Higher Power, we have found sobriety.

We begin the healing process by sharing with them the basis of our journey from darkness to light. That's the key, the icebreaker—you tell your story and then get them to tell theirs. It's that simple.

THE FIVE Cs

The heart of the Twelfth Step call is when we share our story: what it was like when we were drinking or using, what happened to make us realize we were sick and needed help, and what it is like now that we have found recovery through working a Twelve Step program. This formula has been the key to passing on the Twelve Step miracle since 1935 and is why I opened this book with my own story. This process is outlined in the Big Book in the chapter "Working with Others" and can be subdivided into five parts, summarized by the five Cs: Confidence, Confession, Conviction, Conversion, and Continuance. Though these terms aren't used, the parts are outlined in detail from pages 90 to 100 in the Big Book. In these passages, Bill W. eloquently lays out a model of talking points for us to follow during our Twelfth Step calls.

The first thing to do when trying to help others is to gain their *Confidence*—the establishment of rapport between the Twelfth Stepper and the prospect, which is outlined on page 91 of the Big Book. We do this by first engaging in general conversation, sharing something about ourselves, and learning a little about the other person. We then begin the "what it was like" part of our stories, sharing honestly and without rancor, remorse, or reservation how we drank and how we used.

Dr. Bob tells us that Bill W. was the first person he had ever heard speak so clearly about what he had been going through *from personal experience and so he listened to Bill and trusted what he had to say.*

My friend Harry W. had this to say about sharing his story during a Twelfth Step call: "After telling my story, they now know I'm an addict and I'm sick like them, which makes the fact that I'm recovered even more amazing. Now they trust me and I've got their full attention. The fact that they know I'm just like them makes me qualified to talk to them. Otherwise I'm just like a normal person like their parents, doctor, or therapist, who they never listen to."

The next phase of discussion is *Confession,* outlined on pages 91 and 92 of the Big Book. This is where we continue the "what it was like" portion of our story by talking about the troubles our drinking caused and how we went against our morals and hurt other people, even after promising time and again that we would quit. We tell how our mental craving and obsession would inevitably bring us back to the same out-of-control drinking and using, and cause further harm and suffering. It may help to share some more humorous escapades to connect with prospects and to get them to share their stories as well.

We "confess" also by sharing the obstacles that had prevented us from recovering. If we have gained their confidence, our prospects will also begin to share their troubles in more intimate detail and unburden their soul.

This brings us to *Conviction,* described on pages 92 and 93 of the Big Book. This is the mental process by which the prospect becomes aware of the nature of his or her faults, and learns that there is hope for overcoming them. This begins the "what happened" part of our story, where we talk about how we had to face the hopelessness of this disease. We mention that this is usually what led us to the solution of deciding to turn our lives over to a Power greater than ourselves, stressing that each of us must find our own definition of that Power. We then talk about the Big Book's program of action, including how we admitted our faults and straightened out our past so that we can now be helpful to others in order to stay sober.

With *Conversion* we begin to talk about the "what it's like now" part of our story—a conversion that is based on a commitment to follow our Higher Power's guidance. You'll find the instructions for this on pages 95 to 98 in the Big Book.

If we succeeded in gaining our prospects' confidence and our talk has landed on fertile soil, our new friends will have voluntarily shared their own story with us, made an admission of their power-lessness and the consequences of their active disease, and may be ready to believe in a Power greater than themselves. If so, they will have taken the first two Steps.

If Dr. Bob were your Twelfth Step call partner, he would take you through the Third Step right then and there, requiring you to get on your knees and "make a surrender to the God of your understanding." For many people, their initial surrender can mean anything from a willingness to work the rest of the Steps to a com-mitment to let their Higher Power—however they define that—replace their drug-obsessed ego in guiding their decisions. It is essential that they make that Step Three decision as early on as possible to be able to move on to Step Four.

No matter what, I leave a copy of the Big Book and my phone number, and make plans to visit again the following day and every day after that, so long as my new prospect remains willing. That brings us to the fifth C and the next phase in the Twelfth Step call, *Continuance,* which strengthens and reaffirms conversion through ongoing guidance and support. Information on that is found on page 100 of the Big Book: "Both you and the new man must walk day by day in the path of spiritual progress."

Continuance means we make a commitment to our prospect. Without ongoing commitment on our part, they will likely not make it and we will be employing only half measures. Our job is not finished simply by a single conversation or dropping them off at the detox and popping in and having a brief chat. We stay with them until they have understood that addiction is a disease, that they have this disease—or at least believe they may have it—and that working a Twelve Step program offers a solution to their suffering.

Eventually you turn them over to the group, where they commit to finding a sponsor (whether it's you or someone else) and continuing to work through the Steps. It's important that they find groups where they feel supported and that are compatible—not every meeting is right for everybody. Some people respond to a Big Book meeting, others to a speaker or Step meeting. Factors such as age, gender, sexual orientation, and cultural or racial origin may play a part in their decision to commit to a home group. The formula of ninety meetings in ninety days is a good one for new people, who are especially vulnerable to relapse—or for people who are coming off a relapse. It's a way for people to attend a variety of meetings, which can provide a robust support network for them as they make their commitment to the program. You can expedite this by doing some research, going to meetings with them, and helping them select groups that will best meet their needs.

When they have worked their way to Step Twelve, the cycle is complete and they then start sponsoring others and living the life of service that their spiritual awakening makes possible. Our collective continued sobriety is ensured only by the continued growth of our fellowship, made possible through our collective commitment to passing on to others what has been given to us.

Opportunities to carry the message will pop up often and without warning, so be prepared to respond quickly, bearing in mind that the eventual goal of our Twelfth Step call is to get the person involved in the Twelve Step community, where they will find the guidance and support they need to work through the Twelve Steps. I recently asked my friend Wally P. how much time he thought we have to complete the full Step Twelve process. He said, "When a sick and suffering friend reaches out to the Twelve Step community for help, whether from a treatment center, detox, from home, a bar, or from the street, he or she passes through a brief window of opportunity—a time when he or she is most teachable. How much time do we have to alleviate this pain? Do we have a year? Absolutely not! Do we have a month? Sometimes we do, sometimes we don't. Do we have a week? For many, that may be pushing it. What if we only have today? What if we assume the newcomer is going to relapse tomorrow (in many cases this is true)? Remember—this is life and death."

You will be able to fine-tune your Twelfth Step skills and bolster your confidence through also studying the Big Book chapters "To Wives," "The Family Afterward," and "To Employers." You can gain additional experience and guidance through sponsorship, riding shotgun on Twelfth Step calls, learning from the experience of older members, and attending Step Twelve workshops.

MAKING A TWELFTH STEP CALL IN A NUTSHELL

To further assist you with your Twelfth Step call, I have put together a list of twelve simple suggestions that I hope will make your job easier and increase your chances of success. These guidelines were culled from personal experience and from my research and reading over the years.

1. If the call for help comes over the telephone, call back immediately. Arrange a time and place to meet, and show up on time.

2. Twelfth Step calls are most effective when the prospect is sober or fairly sober. Carrying our message to intoxicated

alcoholics rarely works. They may not even be conscious that you are with them because of blackouts. Wait for the end of a spree or for a lucid interval when the prospect is still jittery—there is nothing more valuable to aid you in your work than a prospect with the gift of desperation.

3. You may be called by someone while they are sitting in a bar. The first painful lesson learned by Bill W. and Dr. Bob was to never talk to a drunk about sobriety while they are drinking in a bar. Go to the bar only to pick the person up and, preferably, to get him or her to a detox or to a meeting, and do your work after they have sobered up.

4. If this is your first Twelfth Step call, go with your sponsor or someone experienced. If at all possible, make your Twelfth Step call in pairs, preferably with someone of the same gender. Twelfth Step calls are often emotionally intense and can sometimes become physically intense— there is safety in numbers and two heads are better than one. Should violence seem imminent, leave. If necessary, call the police.

5. Dress your best. Remember that if the one who is suffering is new to our way of life, you will stand in their mind as a symbol, representing your Twelve Step fellowship and program.

6. During home calls, separate your prospect from family if you can. The family members are usually so enmeshed in the addict's drinking or using, they can be distracting and even disruptive to the process. Learn from experienced AAs how to interact with family or significant others on the scene. You will soon be able to keenly discern when it is wiser to leave than to remain and debate with the family if they insist on being involved.

7. Suggest detox and rehab if needed, and make appropriate arrangements with family or significant others if the prospect is willing to go.

8. Share your personal story detailing your own drinking habits, active addiction, and recovery. Keep the focus on you. Remember, don't moralize, lecture, or brand prospects as alcoholics or addicts. That conclusion is theirs to make.

9. Share your understanding of the disease of alcoholism; let the person know that this disease is progressive and can end with insanity or early death. Describe the conditions of body, mind, and spirit that accompany alcoholism and addiction to other drugs. Share exactly what happened to you.

10. The prospect will probably want to know how long you have been recovered and how you got and stayed clean and sober. Include that when you share your Twelve Step recovery experience. Tell them how Twelve Step recovery has worked for you and helped you regain your sanity while maintaining sobriety, how it has led to being willing to believe in a Power greater than yourself. Use common, secular language to avoid arousing prejudice against theological terms and conceptions. Remember that our solution is a spiritual solution, not a religious one. The spiritual part of our program is like the wet part of the ocean, so learn to talk about it.

11. Share with your prospect how your life is today. Talk about your recovery program as not just giving up drinking and using, but the start of a challenging, rewarding way of living that has replaced the false promises of alcohol and other drugs with a renewed sense of hope and self-worth.

12. Leave a meeting schedule, a Big Book, Twelve Step recovery pamphlets, and your phone number, and make at least one follow-up visit or phone call. Offer to return for further questions and help with transportation to a meeting, if possible. Mention that Al-Anon meetings are available to family members and significant others.

The Big Book reminds us that, despite our best efforts, not everyone wants what we have or is willing to go to any length to get it.

> Do not be discouraged if your prospect does not respond at once. Search out another alcoholic and try again. You are sure to find someone desperate enough to accept with eagerness what you offer. We find it a waste of time to keep chasing a man who cannot or will not work with you. If you leave such a person alone, he may soon become convinced that he cannot recover by himself. To spend too much time on any one situation is to deny some other alcoholic an opportunity to live and be happy. (*Alcoholics Anonymous* 2001, 96)

We live in a world where drugs and alcohol have become among the greatest threats to human health and sanity. Within earshot of where you are reading this book, there is probably an alcoholic or addict who is literally dying for what you have. If you are willing to sign up for this lifesaving service, your Higher Power will certainly present you with wonderful, astonishing opportunities to grow spiritually as you practice the art of the Twelfth Step call. When you become ready, willing, and able to live as a Twelfth Step soldier, buckle your seatbelt, fasten your chin strap, and prepare to be rocketed into the fourth dimension of living.

7

The Joys and Gifts of Sponsorship

❧❦❧

No one reaps full benefit from any fellowship he is connected
with unless he wholeheartedly engages in its important
activities. . . . Any A.A. who has not experienced the joys and
satisfaction of helping another alcoholic regain his place in
life has not yet fully realized the complete benefits of this fellow-
ship. . . . Until an individual has assumed the responsibility
of setting a shaking, helpless human being back on the path
toward becoming a healthy useful, happy member of society,
he has not enjoyed the complete thrill of being an A.A.

Clarence H. S., 1944

Having made our initial contact by conducting some form of a
Twelfth Step call—assuming we have found a prospect who is truly
an alcoholic or an addict, and provided that our prospect knows
it and wants our help—our job then is to sponsor our new friend
into our fellowship and introduce them to our way of life by getting
them to meetings and taking them through the Steps. Eventually,
the goal is to help them understand the critical importance of giving
of ourselves in service to others. Sometimes, our prospect will find
a sponsor in one of their meetings that is a better fit and is more
available to support them over the long haul; when this happens,
we gladly support them in that transition. Through sponsorship,

whether with a prospect or with people who we encounter in meetings, we give of our time and our experience in the hope that our
sponsees will become spiritually fit and fully vested members of
our society and will, in turn, pass it on to others and continue the
cycle of healing.

The complete benefits of Step Twelve are not fully available to
us unless we work intensively with others, and sponsorship is one
of the most effective and rewarding ways to do this.

Anyone who is truly successful in Alcoholics Anonymous or
any Twelve Step fellowship is someone who is able to achieve quality long-term recovery, which is marked by having a sense of joy,
well-being, peace, and general contentment. Those who are most
successful understand the vital principle of giving without expectation of reward and that the complete benefits of Step Twelve are
not fully available to us unless we work intensively with others.
Sponsorship is one of the most effective and rewarding pathways to
achieve this high-quality and lasting recovery. Twelve Step recovery
is not a self-help program—it is a "we help one another" program.
Anyone who has completed the first eleven Steps has those eleven
tools for achieving sobriety to give away and is qualified to become
a sponsor.

For me, serving newcomers as a sponsor is like taking medication that annihilates the ever-present virus of selfishness that
lingers in my DNA that, left untreated, will become virulent again,
drive me to drink and drugs, and eventually destroy me. Sponsorship forces me to self-check my program on a daily basis, and that
is my insurance policy against becoming a dangerous egomaniac
once again.

Each time I sponsor a newcomer, I magically seem to acquire
another ounce of emotional sobriety. My sense of abundance and
peace increases. It is the gift we give ourselves that keeps on giving
in every aspect of our lives and is a key to our ability to remain
comfortably clean and sober.

HOW I LEARNED TO BE A SPONSOR

At first glance, becoming a sponsor seemed like a tall order. I had to become willing to face my sloth and natural selfishness. And, to become a good sponsor, I needed to study the Big Book a bit in order to quell my worries that I would say or do the wrong thing. Most importantly, I had to truly turn over my ego to the care of my Higher Power. Due to my own sponsor's insistence, I put on my big boy pants and made the decision to do whatever it took to practice this vital aspect of Step Twelve by doing the work that is mine to do as a full member of our society.

Right out of the gate, working with my first sponsee, I discovered a level of joy that I had never known, and instantly my fears of incompetence vanished.

I was told to choose my first sponsee, just as my sponsor—an old-school AA whose father had been sponsored by Bill W. in Brooklyn, New York—had chosen me. My sponsor learned from those early pioneers that the sponsors needed to choose who they were going to sponsor. He taught me that the newcomer is lost, that finding anything at that stage is a monumental task, and most are not likely to ask someone to sponsor them on their own.

Each time I was discharged from a treatment center, the clinical staff urged me to return to my home, go to meetings, and find a sponsor who had what I wanted. I had no clue what I wanted from sponsor. What I wanted at the time was a job, a new place to live, a tan, a love interest, whiter teeth, and money. And I wanted someone to show me how to safely continue using drugs and drinking. I was the quintessential newcomer. Lost. Sick in mind, body, and spirit. Not only lacking social skills, but terrified, angry, and confused to boot.

It was impossible for me to ask someone for help at that time, especially at the level of what I understood sponsorship to be. I saw the sponsor as some kind of 24/7 mentor, and asking for that kind of commitment was like asking somebody to marry me, which I didn't have a very good track record with. That track record played out when I made the mistake of impulsively deciding to choose my sponsor without really knowing anything about the person and what the qualifications were for sponsorship.

At my first meeting out of treatment, a very well-dressed man entered the room, wearing Armani, a precision haircut, and an expensive watch and shoes. He laughed a lot, and everyone hugged him and seemed to like him. He appeared happy and prosperous, and during his sharing I learned that he lived at a very fancy address. During his share he quoted a few times from the Big Book.

I thought to myself, okay, this guy has what I want. After the meeting I steeled up my nerve and asked him to become my sponsor. He said that we would have to get to know one another first. He invited me to his place for coffee, and then he asked me if I lived nearby. He suggested that on the way to his apartment we should stop by my place so I could grab a toothbrush and change of clothes in case we started working Steps, which he said might go on into the wee hours. I was intrigued by the idea of working the Steps, which I had heard so much about during my stay at the dual diagnosis treatment center, and so I did what I was told.

Shortly after arriving at his apartment, we got into a heated argument over a quote from the Big Book. I did not have a Big Book and insisted that he read me the passage in question in order to settle the argument. He seemed to have misplaced his Big Book, and, after much searching, we found it on the floor in the back of his closet, the pages stuck together from mildew and mold. After reading "The Doctor's Opinion," he said he needed to relax. He then took off his slacks and invited me to watch some porn with him. I grabbed his pants and wallet, and fled into the night. I returned to my place and immediately called a drug dealer.

That night I completely abandoned any hope of ever finding a sponsor for myself. I continued riding the merry-go-round of relapse and treatment. After each subsequent discharge from a treatment program, I made it to a few meetings alone and afraid, sat in the back, and never found anyone who had what I wanted.

Each time, I quickly relapsed, finding lower bottoms on my drug-fueled express train bound for hell.

It was during what would be my last stint in rehab, following the treatment center's regularly scheduled Monday night Twelfth Step call, that my first sponsor chose me. For this I am eternally grateful. This wonderful man placed his hand in mine and spared me untold additional trips to detox, failed treatment, and eventual death.

My first sponsor did it the old-fashioned way—he chose his "pigeons" and raised them up 1940s style. From the beginning, he instilled in me the importance of service and working with others. He took me through the Steps quickly and as often as was needed until I got them. He taught me that the Big Book was a textbook, a training manual for both sponsees and sponsors, and suggested that I find a second sponsor in case he wasn't available and to get an expanded point of view of the program—two heads being better than one. He explained that we meet as equals, and then would always laugh and say, "Well, we aren't equals just yet, but we soon will be." He laughed easily and was serenity personified.

Through working the first eleven Steps with him quickly, I did experience a radical shift in my awareness, an opening up of my heart—the spiritual awakening promised in the Big Book. But for me, the most profound healing miracle of my recovery happened the first time I reached out my hand with no expectation of personal gain and informed another alcoholic that I was going to become his sponsor.

I had just completed my first pass through the first eleven Steps. One of my sponsors informed me that I could now sign up as a member of his home group, which I felt compelled to do that same evening. When the chairperson made the announcement that our home group promotes sponsorship and asked all members willing to be a sponsor to please raise their hands, everyone in the room did except for me. I was the only newcomer, and considering how many hands were raised, I figured the rest of the group had it covered and didn't need any help from me.

My sponsor called me out right there at the meeting in front of everyone. He looked at me and snapped, "You've done your Steps—how can you be a home group member and not be willing to sponsor? What kind of message does that send out to a newcomer?"

After the meeting ended, I was told in no uncertain terms that I was now expected to find myself a newcomer to serve. It was strongly suggested that I attend several meetings every day, and at each meeting my service work would be to appoint myself as a group greeter in order to get to know as many people as possible. I was told to look for someone who was new and in pain, and offer to become his sponsor.

It was burned into my mind that this was now my job—the spiritual dues that I must pay to maintain my seat in the rooms of our fellowship. I balked. The very thought of becoming a sponsor made me uneasy. I didn't feel like I knew enough about the program to begin teaching it to someone else, but my sponsor insisted. He admonished me: "Selfishness is the root of our troubles—we have got to get rid of it or it kills us! You've got to do this if you want to grow and stay well and be happy in recovery. You cannot just sit there at meetings and soak it up and take and take and take and not give back."

I did as I was told. I wanted to stay clean and sober more than anything and had become completely willing to be a good Twelfth Step soldier. I was emboldened by having read through the first 164 pages of the Big Book, having completed the Steps, and having accompanied my sponsors on numerous Twelfth Step calls during my first ninety days of sobriety.

That night in bed, before doing my Tenth Step, I skimmed through "Working with Others," "How It Works," and "The Doctor's Opinion" in the Big Book, in anticipation of taking on my first sponsee. In my prayers I told God that I was ready, and asked Him to please send me someone to sponsor if He agreed with me.

The following evening, before heading out to one of my favorite meetings, I decided to wear something cheerful, knowing that that would be my first stab at serving as greeter at the meeting, on the hunt for my first sponsee.

I chose to wear a bright yellow polo shirt, a bright yellow Windbreaker, brown corduroy jeans, and white sneakers. Earlier that day, I had met up with a new friend in the program who was studying cosmetology and allowed her to streak my hair with bleach. My sponsor told me that it looked like my hair had picked up a drink and had turned me into a human daisy.

I arrived at the meeting space thirty minutes early in order to take my position at the door and stand at the ready to shake the hand of everyone who entered. I was the first person at the meeting. I set up all the chairs in a circle and sat by the door and eagerly waited.

I heard the outer door open and close followed by heavy footsteps coming toward the door. The doorknob turned, but the door didn't open. Then I heard footsteps again walking away from the door. I glanced out of the window. There was a man of a certain age pacing back and forth smoking a cigarette. He was clearly distraught and had tears in his eyes. He was wearing a three-piece suit, a Rolex, expensive shoes, and carrying a briefcase. I saw him take a deep breath and enter the building, and once again I could hear his heavy footsteps approaching the door to the meeting room.

I jumped up and took my position. He opened the door with force—his eyes were watery and bloodshot. His tear-stained face was puffy and ruddy, his nose a riot of gin blossoms. I have never seen anyone who looked so sad and hollow. A shell of a man stood before me, as desperate as only the dying can be. I positively sizzled with zeal. I beamed and stuck out my hand and said, "Hi, I'm Gary, I'm a recovering alcoholic. Are you new to AA, or are you just new to me?"

He stared, mouth open, eyes filled with terror.

Again I thrust out my hand and said, "Welcome to the Powerless Group. What's your name?"

Suddenly he did an about-face, slammed the door in my face, and bolted out of the building. I thought about it for a few seconds, grabbed a scrap of paper and scribbled my phone number on it, and ran out the door in hot pursuit. I made a decision that this man was going to become my sponsee. I was just certain that he needed my help. If there had been a butterfly net in that room, I would have grabbed it before running after him. I chased him all the way across West Forty-Third Street in Manhattan, from Tenth Avenue to Eighth Avenue. He kept looking backward over his shoulder, absolutely horrified by the sight of being chased by a sober human daisy.

When he finally ran out of breath and slowed down, I caught up to him. I handed him my phone number. He stared at me. I said, "Hey, don't be afraid. I ran away from my first meeting. It's OK. Give me a call if you ever want to get sober. I got sober three months ago. This thing really works, and I would be glad to show you how we do it."

He very quietly thanked me for trying to help and quickly walked away. I watched as he ducked into a Blarney Stone Pub on Eighth Avenue in Hell's Kitchen. I couldn't help myself. I followed him into the bar. Just before he ordered a drink, I plopped down next to him on a barstool.

He was aghast. I said, "Hey, I don't mean to be rude, but I never did find out your name. May I know your name?" He told me that his name was Alex. The bartender asked what we were having, and my prospect looked at me and shrugged. He kept eyeing the door, no doubt planning his escape as I ordered two Cokes. We sat silently next to one another, smoking and drinking our Cokes.

He looked me square in the eye, and with tears running down his face, he told me that booze was killing him and that he was so lonely and depressed that he wanted to die. I suggested we go for a walk, and together we ended up at a small park on West Forty-Third Street, just down the street from where the meeting was.

For about thirty minutes, I shared with him about why I go to meetings and about how I met my sponsor and how he took me through the Twelve Steps and what I got out of it. He listened intently, never taking his eyes off mine. He apologized for making me miss the meeting. I looked at my watch and cheerfully announced that there was still time to catch the last half of the meeting and suggested that we hurry back to the Powerless Group.

After the meeting, he asked if I would go with him to the diner for some coffee. We talked for a couple hours, during which time, to the best of my ability, I Twelfth Stepped him the way I had observed my sponsor do it during his Twelfth Step calls. I shared my story. I talked about our spiritual solution and the Step work that I did with my sponsor. I told him how much better my life had become in only three months.

I asked him to tell me his story. I listened to him without interruption, except to laugh and nod and say, "been there" and "uh-huh, me too" and "I did that also." I told him about some of my crazier escapades, which made him howl with laughter. He said he had never thought he would laugh again.

I seized the moment and invited him to join us in AA and try our way of life. I offered to sponsor him and show him the way out as it was given to me. He halfheartedly agreed. I suggested that he call me anytime during the night if he felt like he needed to drink and committed to see him the next day at the same meeting.

He did call me twice that night, and he called again the next afternoon and at 7:00 p.m. that evening. I went early to the Powerless Group carrying two Big Books, and lo and behold, my prospect showed up.

After the meeting, we went to the diner and then to the park on West Forty-Third and began reading through the Big Book. We met each evening for the next week—I took him to various meetings, and after each meeting we would go to a diner for coffee and continue our Big Book study. During those sessions, together we completed Steps One, Two, and Three.

On the weekend, I introduced him to my sponsor, and the three of us worked Steps Four, Five, Six, Seven, and Eight. Any questions he had for me that I didn't know the answer to, I deferred to my sponsor.

The following week we finished reading the first 164 pages of the Big Book. I was astonished how really easy the whole process was—a sober monkey could have done it!

Did I take him through the process perfectly? Not likely, but God took care of both of us: Alex stayed sober and I stayed sober. Each time I gave of myself in service to my sponsee, remarkable events began to unfold in my life—the perks we receive as a benefit of having a new Employer who is all powerful.

Alex continued to work with me. I suggested that he find a second sponsor, which he did. At ninety days sober, he took on his first sponsee, just as I had done. His life began to transform rapidly—which seems to happen as a direct result of fully embracing the Step Twelve way of living. Our lives take on new meaning, sometimes quickly, sometimes slowly.

Alex quickly became a service warrior and gave back to the group. He continued to sponsor other men, taking them through the Steps as fast and often as needed, keeping the process simple. He became a philanthropist in sobriety and helped many men and women get into treatment and turn their lives around.

As a direct result of his commitment to live in maximum service by practicing a thorough and ongoing Twelfth Step, his standing in the business community was restored. Once again, he was able to resume his role as a trusted member of the law firm he worked at, and his relationships with family were all healed. His life became filled with love and laughter and peace. To watch that happen with the knowledge that I had planted in his mind and heart the first seeds of his sobriety gave me the greatest joy. Chasing Alex down the street and extending my hand in sponsorship was a watershed moment in my recovery, a moment that sent my life on an entirely new trajectory of love and service.

On his second anniversary, Alex shared his experience, strength, and hope during our home group speaker meeting and brought me to tears of laughter and joy when he spoke so gratefully about the night he was Twelfth Stepped by a "bat-shit crazy human daisy" who chased him through midtown Manhattan and saved his life.

Alex never drank again. The day he passed away from lung cancer, he died sober.

I was probably a lousy sponsor at first. But I did have things to offer that are available to us all—my enthusiasm, my strength, my hope, and my love. I also learned a valuable lesson: If somebody wants to stay sober, there's almost nothing you can say to wreck that for them. All we have to do is show up for them and bring our own recovery—and demonstrate our sobriety by "walking the talk," so no matter what we say, we *wear* the message.

SPONSORSHIP 101

If you are ready to discover the most profound gift that Step Twelve has to offer, and you're not already a sponsor, then it's time for you to find a sponsee. In our sick and suffering world, we can find a newcomer in need of help almost anywhere we turn. Certainly anytime that we find a willing prospect at a meeting or during all manner of Twelfth Step calls, we are gifted with a perfect opportunity to ramp up our recovery by offering ourselves in service as a sponsor.

There are as many sponsorship styles as there are alcoholics and addicts in recovery. Becoming a sponsor requires commitment, and the job comes with certain responsibilities. Here are a few suggestions to keep in mind as you prepare to take on those responsibilities and begin "giving it away to keep it" by powerfully incorporating a dynamic Twelfth Step into your life:

- Have your own sponsor (preferably two), and stay in close contact with them when you begin working with a newcomer.

- Work the first eleven Steps yourself, and revisit them as often as needed.

- Study the first 164 pages of the Big Book with your sponsor and other experienced members of your home group.

- Read AA and other Twelve Step literature on sponsorship, and attend any available circuit speaker sessions and workshops on the topic.

- Practice daily prayer and meditation—learn to listen for your Higher Power's guidance in making a decision to sponsor someone and before each work session with your sponsee.

- Don't sponsor someone of the opposite gender (or of the same gender, if you're gay) unless there is no other alternative for that person, in which case avoid anything that is suggestively or overtly romantic or sexual.

- A sponsor is not a therapist. Your job is to help the person work a quality Twelve Step program of recovery. If they need to deal with personal problems not related to their drinking or using, suggest they see their clergy person or a therapist.

- Confidentiality is essential. "What is said here, stays here" applies to your sessions with your sponsee just as it does to meetings.

- Allow your sponsee to define their own Higher Power, and avoid trying to influence them with your spiritual or religious beliefs.

- If a friendship develops outside of your sponsorship relationship, be careful to not let that compromise your objectivity in helping your sponsee work a rigorous program. If you think that could happen, help them find another sponsor.

- Be available to your sponsee as much as possible, but don't overpromise—if you aren't able to be on call 24/7, let them know when you are available and what you're willing to do. If you're going to miss an appointment or be late, let them know.

- Avoid financial involvement, either in lending or borrowing money or being involved in each other's business deals. Things were different back in the 1930s and 1940s, when the early AAs would provide financial support to their prospects. More social and treatment services are available now that you can help your sponsee access.

- Daily, ask God to remove from your heart and mind any obstacles that block your ability to be of maximum service.

- Never talk down to your sponsee; treat them with dignity and respect, and remember that your sponsees are helping you stay sober as much as you are helping them.

Being fearful of sponsorship is nothing more than False Evidence Appearing Real. If you are apprehensive about the time commitment of sponsorship, remember that we always had time to acquire and use alcohol and other drugs, so we can make sponsorship one of our priorities for working Step Twelve to stay sober. If you can only sponsor one person, that's better than none; simply work with as many people as you effectively can. We don't have to try to be a Dr. Bob, who sponsored five thousand men through the Steps, but there is always time if we make the time.

If you are apprehensive about taking a sponsee through the Steps for the first time, pocket your pride and ask your sponsor or another experienced recovery partner to help. Each time we guide a newcomer through the Steps, we grow in ways that are mind-boggling.

Over time I have developed a step-by-step outline that I share with my sponsees to use as a handy guide as they embark on the most thrilling adventure of their sober life—the day they sit down with their first sponsee, read through the first 164 pages of the Big Book, and show them what the Twelve Steps are all about. This is my approach. You will find your own and will learn to modify it depending on the person you're sponsoring.

If he is able to focus and read, then we take turns reading. If not, I do the reading:

- Read through the title page, the foreword, and the preface—take time to discuss what you are reading.

- Read "The Doctor's Opinion."

- Read "Bill's Story."

- Read "There Is a Solution."

- Read "More about Alcoholism," then back up and take them through Step One.

- Read "We Agnostics," then back up and take them through Step Two.

Depending on how shaky my sponsee is, that may be all he is able to handle for the first session, but I do my best to get him through to Step Three in the first session.

- Read "How It Works." When we come to the Third Step prayer on page 63, I ask him to think about what that prayer means, and we pray the Third Step prayer together.

- We continue with "How It Works" and create a simple Fourth Step chart using the model shown on page 65; the first time I take my sponsee through the Fourth Step, I ask him questions and fill out the chart for him. We don't belabor it—we're thorough but we keep it simple, following the Big Book's directions. (There are a lot of good Fourth Step guides you might want to look into as well—see the resources section in the back of this book for a recommendation.)

- In a separate session, we begin reading the chapter "Into Action," and we take the Fifth Step, following the instructions in the Big Book for him to listen for his Higher Power, having completed the Fifth Step.

- In our next session, we continue reading through "Into Action" as we take Steps Six, Seven, and Eight. We make his amends list in preparation for him to begin making his Ninth Step amends immediately.

- Next session, we begin Steps Ten, Eleven, and Twelve, reading through "Working with Others," "To Wives," "The Family Afterward," and "To Employers."

- Once he has reached Step Twelve, we make it clear that the matter of giving back is not in question but rather when and how.

When I sponsor a newcomer, we try to complete this process within his first thirty days of sobriety. When he reaches ninety days clean and sober, we celebrate by asking his Higher Power to send him someone he can sponsor.

Does this sound like a lot of hard work? The first couple of times it might feel that way, but we get used to it. We accept this work as part of our life in Twelve Step recovery. If we are not working this Step, then we have not made a full commitment to Twelve Step recovery. If you do nothing else but help a sponsee discover the miraculous gift contained in the first 164 pages of the Big Book, you will have helped them beyond measure, and your own recovery will mature to new levels of spiritual empowerment.

In Step Twelve—the culmination of the preceding Steps— Bill W. asks us to practice spiritual principles in all of our affairs. Sponsorship is the golden opportunity to learn how to put those spiritual principles into action.

STEP TWELVE WARRIORS TOPIC MEETING: SPONSORSHIP

In the course of writing this book, I have depended on the wisdom of a number of Step Twelve warriors, and I'll close this chapter with a virtual topic meeting on sponsorship, with several of them sharing how sponsorship has transformed their programs by giving them a powerful tool for living in Step Twelve.

Welcome to the Step Twelve Warriors group of Alcoholics Anonymous. My name is Gary K., and I'm grateful that I have recovered from the disease of alcoholism and addiction—contingent upon daily maintenance of my spiritual condition.

The topic of our meeting today is the benefits of sponsorship.

Wally P.—*alcoholic from Tucson, Arizona*

Thanks to the spiritual solution found through Twelve Step recovery, it is no longer necessary for me to take a drink or a drug or overeat in order to find peace.

Well, naturally, whenever I sponsor someone, I invariably take them through the Steps, and at some juncture during the journey, they're going to say something that's going to trigger something that's been either buried in the deep, dark recesses of my unconscious mind that I had never inventoried, or they are going to have a different perspective on the healing process that is very insightful and different from the way I had been thinking. They help ME to grow, and they cause me to have incredible epiphanies.

Carver B.—*from Hattiesburg, Mississippi—sober since 2004*

I am a grateful alcoholic in long-term recovery, and I have found the joy of living through service.

Believe me when I tell you that everybody in recovery needs a newcomer in their life. I need to be reminded, through the eyes of another man, about the reality of the pain of our disease and the miracle of recovery, and when I see the desperation and I feel the pain that they are in, and I take them through the Steps and see them slowly transforming before my eyes, it makes an entirely new and holy reality out of recovery. I want and need to experience that over and over and over again.

Randy F.—*grateful recovered drunk from Southport, North Carolina—sober since May 2, 1985*

Recently I suffered kidney failure, and while waiting for a kidney to be donated, I had to begin the arduous and often painful process of dialysis. I began to feel sorry for myself and isolate. After three decades of recovery, I knew exactly what I needed to get me out of my own head, give me strength, and help me to heal. And it started with a prayer: "OK, God, I really feel like I need this—a newcomer to work with, someone who will demand a lot of my time and require me to really make an effort and expend energy. I need to make a commitment to really show up for someone else who needs help. It would do me good, and if they are willing, I think that I could do them some good by carrying the message. I need the spiritual booster shot, and I know that you will give me the strength and the power to carry out the work."

I continued to say that prayer every morning for the next few days, and at the end of the week while sitting at a meeting, this guy walked in the door fresh out of detox, sick and suffering. So I walked up and greeted him, offered him coffee, and made him feel welcome. I passed around our local meeting directory to get phone numbers from the men in our group. I shared at the meeting, which happened to be on the topic of working with others.

At one point during our meeting, our chairperson asked for a show of hands from anyone with a year or more sober who is willing to be a sponsor. I looked right at the newcomer as I raised my hand.

After the meeting, just as I was about to offer to become his sponsor, the newcomer walked right up to me and told me that he liked what I had to say and respected my program, such as he knew of it, and he mentioned that he noticed I had raised my hand and asked me to become his sponsor.

Jody K.—*recovering alcoholic and addict from Minneapolis, Minnesota*

I'm so grateful to be at this meeting.

I become a better person through sponsoring because it forces me to become more generous and think about others and put their needs above my wants, and that keeps me sober and brings peace to my heart.

John S.—*alcoholic, overeater, and recovering Al-Anon from Canton, Ohio*

Sponsoring someone is never an imposition. I remember back to how much time was given to me and how patient my first sponsor was with me as I was going through those first months of recovery—majorly low and difficult times in my life. So today I am always willing to give my time. It doesn't really take much—half hour or twenty minutes or fifteen minutes to talk to somebody who desperately needs to be heard and comfort them by sharing my experience. From that work I get such an enormous sense of accomplishment, and it is actually a sense of honor knowing that people are willing to trust me and want to share with me whatever it was that was going on with them that is causing them pain. That's just a beautiful way to live.

Gil M.—*alcoholic from Girard, Pennsylvania—sober since 1987*

I was a schoolteacher for many years. Teaching the Steps to other women was the most important class I ever taught. It's a lifesaving curriculum. As I taught sponsees to rely on the Steps and God in order to recover, I had a deep, personal epiphany that I was not the center of the universe and woke up to an entirely new understanding of humility. That awakening—which came as a result of becoming a sponsor—led me into the ministry. The gifts of sponsorship are for me profound and life changing.

Bobby Z.—*a real alcoholic from Fort Myers, Florida, formerly of Brooklyn, New York—sober since December 15, 1984*

Sponsorship is a critical element of Step Twelve, which helps me guard against being a selfish dry drunk, and that's just one of the benefits I get from Step Twelve service.

I've been sponsoring guys for over thirty years. First of all, if you're out here sober at the meetings and somebody helped you get sober and took you through the Steps and you're not sponsoring people, you are being selfish. You are just coming to the meetings and you are taking your sobriety and you are not willing, by example, to pass it on to somebody else. Why wouldn't you want to sponsor somebody? If I am not sponsoring, then I haven't reaped the full benefits of Step Twelve. Most of the time when members don't sponsor, it's because they are afraid, and the whole point of opening up spiritually is to trust God and banish fear in favor of faith.

There is a feast at the table of recovery, and what I am served at that feast is determined by the amount of effort I invest into practicing Step Twelve and working with others. If all I do is work the first eleven Steps, then I'm going to eat hot dogs. That's my feast. That's it. Of course, at that same table, I have the ability to eat filet mignon, if I practice a complete Twelfth Step and intensively work with others.

Alison H.—*a grateful recovering alcoholic from Laguna Beach, California*

I didn't always sponsor, but I do now—a lot. My spiritual awakening brought me to a realization that if I continued being a taker instead of a giver, I would land back in the life that I was in.

I lived the life of a taker for a long time, and I have learned in the deepest part of my soul the importance of giving back as a sponsor. If I take working with others away from the equation, then my recovery is in trouble.

Sponsoring also helped me learn how to establish healthy boundaries. I realized there was trouble in paradise when I started saying yes to everyone who asked me for help. I realized that my ego is still alive and well, and that I am raging with self whenever I say yes to everyone who asks for help and make commitments that I am unable to honor. When I did that, the women I had intended to help stopped receiving the message that they needed and deserved because it became all about the "Ali Show." I needed to hit a level of humility, which required acquiring emotional sobriety—a gift that I ultimately received as a result of being a sponsor out of control.

If someone asks me for help and I am unable, I stay in contact with them until I can redirect them to someone else who can be available to them, and I work hard to find someone who is ready for a new sponsee.

I actually learn more from my sponsees—sometimes more than my own mentors—and we never know what magic is going to be created in the next experience when you are working with another alcoholic. We do not know the outcome; my responsibility here is to show up and then the results are left to God.

Now my sponsees all have sponsees, and they are also continuously talking about recovery. That is how I think Bill W. and Dr. Bob designed our program: if I am working with a sponsor and with sponsees, I am sandwiched in—I am not going anywhere.

Harry W.—*a twenty-seven-year-old recovering alcoholic and drug addict from South Florida*

I couldn't stay sober without sponsoring. As long as I am working closely with newcomers, sponsoring them, and taking them through the Steps and the Big Book, I am I confident that I will not fall back into the insanity described in "The Doctor's Opinion": irritable, restless, dis-content. Working with other recovering former drunks and junkies constantly reminds me of the solution to our problem, and when I'm taking a bunch of guys through the Steps, I am surrounded with my sponsees and I am safe. As long as I stay in the center of the herd and help others achieve sobriety, the magic and spiritual power of our Twelve Step program and way of life will continue to keep me sober and clean and reasonably happy.

Danny F.—*a twenty-three-year-old Step Twelve warrior—clean and sober since 2014*

Sponsorship saved my life. I had tried all the different ways to get clean and sober: changing my diet, changing my location and relationship, marijuana maintenance, going to church, psychiatry, medicine—whatever—didn't work. Nothing worked. I tried treatment a bunch of times, and it helped in the short term, but without a program after treatment, eventually the disease brought me down until I experienced a spiritual awakening as a result of working the Twelve Steps and sponsoring others.

The last time I was in treatment, I decided to do the deal when I got out. I was getting scared because I was about to be discharged. I had about twenty days clean, and I knew that if I didn't get a sponsor right now and work the Steps, I would be dead. Thank God for all those times that I had been to AA and NA meetings while in treatment. A bunch of those guys had given me their numbers, and I called the first few and they couldn't meet up with me for whatever reason, and the first guy that was available became my sponsor. His name is Harry W.

He had given me his number a long time ago and I blew him off, and then I ran into him at a meeting and I said, "Hey, man, sorry for not calling you. Can we still do this Twelve Step deal?" and he said, "No problem, dude, we can start today. Do you want to get down to work for real? Are you serious about this?" I told him my whole life story and what I did, and he told me his, and from there, whatever he asked me to do, I would just do what I could and be honest with him.

I had about thirty days when we started and I completed my Steps when I had about a hundred days clean and sober. Immediately, I started carrying the message and sponsoring guys.

Sponsoring others takes a lot of time, but I do it because, honestly, that impression made on me by my sponsor was huge.

It isn't enough for me to just have an awakening myself. We have to live the spiritual life and help other guys. Sponsorship changed my life and gave me a life worth living, and it would just be a complete waste if I didn't share it with others.

Andrew L.—*a twenty-nine-year-old recovering alcoholic/addict from Delray Beach, Florida—grateful for another day clean and sober*

What I get out of sponsorship is just what it says in "Working with Others" in the Big Book: "the experience that you don't want to miss." Seeing the change in people is really miraculous. I am working with a new guy, and he will say "recovery is stupid—God is stupid," and then six months later that same guy is saying "dear God, please put a sponsee in my life." I have seen that kind of dramatic change again and again.

Only a few months into my recovery, I was at a meeting and I see a kid wearing a Ravens hoodie and he was seriously shot out. I walked up to him and I said, "Hey, I like your hoodie." He mumbled, "Thanks, man," and started to turn away. I can see that he is not in a good space. So I just blurted out, "If you need a sponsor, just give me a call." So he did call, and you know, at first it was the typical new guy in recovery—he thinks that he knows everything, and he's arrogant and shady, and he was just all over the place emotionally.

During the time it took us to go through the first 164 pages of the Big Book and work the Steps, all of that crap just kind of floated out of him, and he underwent a total metamorphosis. In six months this resentful, selfish, childish drug addict/alcoholic turned into a thoughtful, caring, hard-working grown man. Now this guy is one of my best friends. He has sponsees and grand sponsees now. He totally transformed.

When you see that kind of change in the ones that really get a hold of it, and knowing that you were the one who passed the miracle on to them, it is a really cool feeling like nothing else I have ever experienced.

Being a part of that transformative change and serving as a channel of God's healing—that is mind-blowing for this alcoholic and keeps me signing up for more sponsorship service work. It is a really good feeling like nothing else in this world. I sponsor because I love that feeling of being a channel of good, and I also do it because that was what I was told to do in order to stay sober, and it has not failed me yet.

Working with new guys really keeps me sober, because I see the pain of their early sobriety and all of their drama and anger and all of the negativities and the fresh damage and chaos, and it keeps fresh in my mind. I don't envy them, but I empathize with it because I used to be there, and it reminds me that I don't ever want to go back to that dark place.

Today, because of throwing myself headfirst into Step Twelve, I love my recovery, I love my life and my new friends and my connection with God, and I have a gaggle of sponsees who I love working the Steps with. It's the best part of my life, hands down.

John McA.—*a recovering alcoholic from Nashville, Tennessee—by the Grace of God, I am sober since 1983*

In being a sponsor, I found out what Twelve Step recovery is really about. Sponsorship is the ultimate antidote to our problem, which is selfishness and self-centeredness. If we are honest with ourselves, we have to admit that the need to keep that in check will never entirely go away, which is why we do this intensive work, one-on-one, face-to-face, giving of our time, experience, strength, and hope—expecting nothing in return. It's a whole new way of living.

Great meeting! Thanks to these Step Twelve warriors for sharing their experience, strength, and hope.

Let's close our meeting now with a moment of silence for all of those sick and suffering alcoholics and addicts out there who stopped at Step Eleven.

8

Carry What Message in All of Our Affairs?

Is sobriety all that we are to expect of a spiritual awakening?
. . . No, sobriety is only a bare beginning; it is only the first
gift of the first awakening. If more gifts are to be received, our
awakening has to go on. And if it does go on, we find that bit
by bit we can discard the old life—the one that did not work—
for a new life that can and does work under any conditions
whatever.

Bill W., December 1957

Step Twelve declares that as *the* result of these Steps, we experience a spiritual awakening that compels us to carry to others our message of a spiritual solution.

When I think of a spiritual experience, I think of Bill W.'s sudden blast of life-changing white light in Towns Hospital. I did not initially have a sudden, blinding spiritual nova—mine was of the educational variety. I did experience a spiritual awakening that was much like the way I wake up in the morning—slowly, one eye opens and then closes. Then the other eye opens and then closes. I begin to stretch, I fight it, and, slowly but surely, eventually I wake up. I fight waking up and fought my spiritual awakening for as long as I could, but I eventually had to face the reality of the day—that in fact there is a God, and that God is working in and through my life to the extent that I follow His will for me and allow Him to make changes in me and through me.

For most of us, our spiritual awakening comes slowly as a result of working the Steps, which lead us to the clear realization and acceptance of the three pertinent ideas found in the Big Book in the beginning of chapter 5:

1. That we were alcoholic and could not manage our own lives
2. That probably no human power could have relieved our alcoholism
3. That God could and would if he were sought

As *the* result of these steps, I awoke to the understanding that it was no longer necessary for me to run my life based on self and fear, fueled by drugs and alcohol. As the result of practicing all twelve of the Steps and surrendering to the Twelve Step way of life, I learned that, so long as I aligned myself with God's will by growing along spiritual lines and living in maximum service—especially by working directly and intensively with other drunks—the compulsion to drink would be lifted forever, contingent upon daily maintenance of my newfound spiritual condition. I was promised that not only would my life get better but that it would transform into something beyond my wildest dreams, and so it has.

I accepted the mandate set for us by Step Twelve and began to do that work, which was mine to do and in a maximum manner— no half measures. The chains that formerly bound up my soul and crippled the circumstances of my life dropped away, and I was set free.

This awakening and the precious gift of knowledge about the spiritual solution, which is developing an intimate relationship with God, was knowledge too exciting to keep to myself. I felt compelled to give it away. Living in our Higher Power's will—however we define that Power—is what keeps us sober. And that means being of maximum service to others. It's all about love and service.

My friend Brave F., sober since 2013, embodies this concept powerfully.

• • •

I believe that having a spiritual awakening is simply becoming aware of a reality that has always been there. I believe that every human being is designed to have purpose, as we are all God's kids and we are placed on Earth to help Him help others. I believe that as a recovering alcoholic I am called to serve a very specific purpose—to meet people when they are at their most broken state, and to reach out my hand and carry the message of finding hope and healing through God.

I am simply doing what every human being is designed to do. But for me, as an alcoholic in recovery, I believe that just a little bit more is expected, because we have lived in darkness and are uniquely qualified to show others who suffer from our common problem how to find the light.

For me, the message we carry is the message of love. There are two forces working here, love and fear. When I am driven by selfishness and fear, I will fall into harm. When I am driven by unconditional love, then my life will fall into place, and everything gets filtered through that.

I know it is a cliché, but in order for me to be able to not only live in the solution but also to grow, I have to give it away. I have to share it. That's how this thing is designed; that's how it works.

• • •

I first met Brave at a treatment center where I work. Brave showed up to share his experience, strength, hope, and full commitment to carry the message through visits to hospitals and institutions. He was accompanied by no less than seventeen young men—his sponsees, grand sponsees, and great grand sponsees—something unheard of for this type of service commitment. Normally, two people show up to speak. But seventeen is unheard of. They were there to support Brave. Through his epic sponsorship, each of these men has come to understand from firsthand experience the vital importance of service and carrying the message.

There are many ways to carry this message: here's how the message was carried to our friend Markey F.

• • •

After white knuckling and not drinking for nearly a month, my nerves were shot. One morning, I called Alcoholics Anonymous, a lady answered, and I said, "Hi, sweetie. I hope that you can help me." The lady said, "Well, maybe I can help. When was the last time you had a drink?" I said, "Twenty-six days ago." She said, "Twenty-six days, that's great." And that was the only time anyone had ever said anything nice to me. I just latched onto her like lapdog.

And I was like, "What do I do, what do I do?," and she told me she would meet me at a noon meeting downtown. So I went to my first AA meeting, and I dressed in all white with lots of jewelry and my hair fixed up, and lots of makeup cause I pictured how they would all be there in their trench coats.

It happened to be next door to a hospital, and as it turns out, that meeting was full of professional people; boy, I was glad that I dressed well.

At the end of the meeting, I asked this lady, "Well, what do I do now?" and she said, "Well, I don't care what you do long as you don't drink." That was a wonderful thing to know, because I had grown up in a very fundamentalist religious home, and she wasn't trying to tell me what to do.

She said there are no rules, just suggestions, and she hands me a Big Book and tells me to take it home and read it. Then she said quickly, "But if you want what I have, you do what I do." So I said, "Okay, so what do I do?" and she said, "Can you ask God for help and not take a drink today?" I said, "I guess so" and she said, "Okay, so ask God for help and you don't take a drink today, and tomorrow I will tell you what to do." I said, "Well, okay."

So I came back the second day, and I said, "Okay, so what do I do now?" And she said, "Can you ask God for help, help another drunk here at the meeting, and not take a drink today?," and I said, "Well, I guess so." She said, "OK, good. So ask God for help, help somebody else, don't take a drink today, come back tomorrow, and I will tell you what to do." I said,

"Well, okay." I wanted to take a drink that night, but I told that lady that I wouldn't and I did not want to hurt her feelings—I thought that I would hurt her feelings if I drank.

So Thursday I go back to the meeting, and I am reading the Big Book and I got to page 151 of "A Vision for You," where it talked about the four horsemen and about frustration and despair. All lonely drinkers will know this and will understand, and I understood because I was so lonely and that is why it hit me in the heart and the Big Book had me.

So I go back the third day, and I say hello to the lady, and I said "What do I do now?" And she said, "Well, can you ask God for help and not take a drink today?," and she is really starting to irritate me now.

I was expecting something really complicated, and she said, "Can you not take a drink today?" And I said, "Listen, you have been telling me that for three days." And she said, "Well, that's all there is to it hon. You don't take a drink today and you come back tomorrow and we'll tell you what to do." And it worked. Eventually, I worked the Steps and never drank again. That gal carried the message to me in a way that I was able to hear it.

• • •

Thank God someone was manning the phones when Markey placed that call, and thank God there was a meeting available and a Big Book available and members of our fellowship available at that meeting to plant the seeds of Markey's recovery. Because that meeting was there, Markey was able to find a sponsor to take her through the Steps, providing her with opportunities to serve others so that she could eventually incorporate the solution into her very breath and build an empowered life lived in maximum service to others.

MAKING STEP TWELVE A FULL-COURSE MEAL

Sponsorship may be considered the highest form of Step Twelve service—as the meat and potatoes of Step Twelve. It is through the sponsorship process and Twelfth Step calls that the nitty-gritty work is accomplished, and we forge our most intimate and spiritual connections with other human beings. However, if we want to enjoy a well-balanced, full-course meal at our spiritual feast, there are other delicious opportunities to directly carry the message, such as speaking at meetings; bringing meetings to hospitals, treatment centers, prisons, and other institutions; and hosting and conducting special Twelve Step educational events, such as Wally P.'s Back to Basics Step workshops, Mike F.'s AA History seminars, and Big Book studies such as "The Big Book Comes Alive."

There are a host of Step Twelve service commitments that support creating a space where the message can be carried, ensuring that our meetings are up and running so that the newcomers can find our fellowship, meet their sponsors who will take them through the Steps, and provide us all with ongoing opportunities to be of service.

Many service commitments can be carried out by newcomers, even before they have completed the first eleven Steps, in order to introduce them to the joys and benefits of service. The solution is always found through action: we change our minds by moving a muscle, and moving our service muscles keeps us spiritually fit. These actions of service for the group help us make a deeper surrender by breaking through our arrogance and showing us new levels of humility. Perhaps most importantly, they help us feel like we are a part of the group by making good connections and feeling that we belong, rather than remaining isolated and feeling terminally unique.

Our meetings are the home of our fellowship. Serving as a greeter, making coffee, bringing the donuts and cookies, setting up and cleaning up the meeting space, procuring the anniversary chips, leading meetings, and giving others rides to meetings—each of these opportunities for service is a wonderful spiritual appetizer that will help the newcomer practice the spiritual principles of focusing their energies on serving the needs of others.

Other service commitments that are of great importance to each group and beyond include:

- Holding office as group secretary, treasurer, or chairperson
- Serving on steering committees for roundups, conventions, retreats, and conferences
- Volunteering for local intergroup phone hotlines and meeting referral services

If we are truly invested in Step Twelve and committed to being of maximum service, then we are doing a combination of these service commitments to supplement our work making Twelfth Step calls and sponsorship. We become a walking Big Book and carry our message by power of example.

"IN ALL OUR AFFAIRS"

When we are able to experience the spiritual gifts of living the Twelfth Step by working with others in AA or other Twelve Step programs, we find that a life of service includes all areas of our lives and begin to learn what "in all our affairs" truly means. These principles are to be applied especially in those areas that generated the resentments and fears that we uncovered in our Fourth Step: in our relationships with our spouses and family members, our romantic relationships and friendships, and our relations at work. Often we are happy to turn over every aspect of our lives to the will of our Higher Power, except when it comes to dealing with financial insecurity.

Our good friend Andrew L. shared with me how his business life finally became a success the day he took action to align his business with his Higher Power's will and apply these spiritual principles even in his business affairs.

• • •

If I am not practicing these principles in all of my affairs, then I am deciding what outcomes are supposed to happen and I am not turning anything over to God.

After being sober for a while—living in Steps Ten, Eleven, and Twelve—it has become increasingly uncomfortable and tough to justify

juggling what I know to be God's will and what is me being selfish, want-
ing more money, more of something . . . more whatever it is.

*I learned this lesson in a visceral way when a friend in the fellowship
called on me to serve as a guest speaker at a meeting. I was asked to share
my experience on the topic of "practicing spiritual principles in all of our
affairs."*

*During that meeting, as I spoke about my situation, I was overcome
by a profound deepening in my trust of God and became clear about how
to resolve the moral crisis that was troubling my business life.*

*As a direct result of doing service at that meeting, I made one of the
biggest decisions I ever made in the life of my company and I completely
threw out everything we had been doing for our business strategy. We had
been operating in a certain way that resulted in making a lot of money
quickly, and how we were doing that was making me uncomfortable.
That old way of doing business did not fit with my new sober spiritual life.*

*When I originally started my company, I did not want to go down the
path of making a lot of easy money. I wanted to make money because we
were providing a needed service, because we had a lot of happy custom-
ers, and because we were conducting business the right way, the cleanest
way possible—that was my original intent.*

*We strayed away from that. We had decided that making money and
being profitable was more important than practicing the principles in all
of our affairs.*

*I had decided that we're going to do it this way because other people
do it this way and make a lot of money, but something had to change if
I was going to stay sober and maintain my spiritual health. I just wasn't
happy with where I was, but how do you stop feeding a financial beast
that produces, and produces well?*

*I decided that I was going to pray about it and hopefully God would
give me a way out where I could still keep my employees—where they can
still have a job and I am not going to be homeless because of it.*

*Though I had not been open to it previously, God had already set up
the answer to my dilemma several months earlier, but I wasn't listening.
Six or seven months before this thing came to a spiritual crisis for me,*

I had bumped into someone—just a "hi, nice to meet with you, can I get your phone number?"

I didn't call him for six months. On the day that I had made the decision in my head to change the way I was doing business and practice spiritual principles truly in all of my affairs, he reached out to me, right out of the blue, at a critical moment when it had become imperative that we do something different. This man told me to use an alternative way of marketing and explained it to me in detail. I thought, "Hmm . . . that's a really crazy idea—and I am certain that it's not going to work," at least in terms of producing the kind of results we had been achieving through less scrupulous means.

I thought, "You know what, anything is going to be better than what we are doing now"—making money hand over fist but feeling that it isn't sober behavior. In order to feel right spiritually, I was willing to let go of whatever amount of money I needed to let go of. But it is very tough to stop feeding something that works and that is extremely profitable.

It didn't make sense at first, but it totally works because we are doing what God wants and with honesty and integrity and greater levels of service. The dividends that have paid out since then in terms of the happiness in my life are remarkable, and you can't put a price on that. And you know, as God would have it—it's also a ton more profitable than before!

Because of that decision, so many more doors have opened and my company has more than doubled in size.

This all happened as a result of doing exactly what the Twelfth Step tells us to do—to practice these principles in all of our affairs. In the long run, everything has just worked out amazing.

• • •

When discerning the perfect spiritual principle to apply in our daily lives and which service commitments are right for us, we must remember that the meetings alone are not our solution, service work alone is not our solution, the Big Book alone is not our solution, our sponsor alone is not our solution, and even the Steps alone are not our solution. These are the tools that lead us to the solution, and the solution is always turning our lives over to the care of the God of our understanding.

We ask our Higher Power what we should do. We get quiet and we listen. Then the real guidance comes, and we take action to be of service to others: that's Step Twelve in a nutshell. If you think of our fellowship as a "society," we have paid the highest dues for any club membership on Earth. We have paid with our sanity, our health, and our very souls. Step Twelve service is the price we pay to retain our seat in the rooms of our fellowship. We will never own our recovery—we can only rent it, and rent is due each day.

What are you being asked to do to give back? What is your Higher Power's will for service in your life?

Whatever it is, then, by God, go and do it.

9

More Will Be Revealed

❧

*To reach more alcoholics, understanding of A.A. and public
good will towards A.A. must go on growing everywhere.
We need to be on still better terms with medicine, religion,
employers, governments, courts, prisons, mental hospitals, and
all enterprises in the alcoholism field. We need the increasing
good will of editors, writers, television and radio channels.
These publicity outlets need to be opened ever wider. [As we'll
see later in this chapter, today we can add the explosion of new
electronic media to this list.]*

Bill W., from *As Bill Sees It* p. 255

Twelve Step recovery was revealed to humanity during the dark
days of the Great Depression—there was a drunk in every family
and a drunk in every doorway. Alcoholism became a national epidemic and the largest killer of Americans.

Once again, we are at a pivotal moment in human history as we
face an unprecedented epidemic of addiction to opioids and prescription drugs, heroin, methamphetamine, cocaine, and a host of
new designer drugs that seem to be rolling down the pipe without
ceasing.

I wrote earlier about the global pandemic of alcoholism
and other drug addictions ravaging communities and families,

destabilizing developing nations and health care systems—and at an increasing cost to society as never before seen in human history. Millions around the globe are still sick and suffering, and have never heard about the healing miracle of Twelve Step recovery.

The statistics are mind-numbing:

- An estimated 21.5 million Americans ages 12 and older had a substance use disorder (addiction) in 2014. (Center for Behavioral Health Statistics and Quality 2015)

- In the same year, an estimated 18,000 adolescents in the United States ages 12 to 17 had heroin use disorders. (Center for Behavioral Health Statistics and Quality 2015)

- Worldwide, over three million people die from harmful alcohol use every year. (World Health Organization 2015)

Clearly members of Alcoholics Anonymous and the other Twelve Step fellowships all need to step up their Twelfth Step game.

With dramatic changes in health care laws, insurance regulations for substance abuse, and the creation of new legislation regulating the funding for recovery education, policymakers are setting in motion the future direction of addiction treatment—policies that will have an impact throughout this century. The pro-pharmaceutical faction will be leading the charge, vying for a larger stake of addiction treatment insurance dollars, often aggressively lobbying against the efficacy of the Twelve Step recovery programs in order to gain a larger market share.

The disease of addiction, including alcoholism, is a three-fold illness of body, mind, and spirit. Medical detox and pharmacology are both essential components during early recovery to stabilize the body. This has become especially true with the increased call for anticraving medications for the treatment of opioid addicts. Dr. William D. Silkworth states in "The Doctor's Opinion" in the Big Book, "Of course an alcoholic ought to be freed from his physical craving for liquor, and this often requires a definite hospital proce-

dure, before psychological measures can be of maximum benefit."
(xxvii–xxviii)

Addiction rehabs provide an invaluable opportunity for our
sick brothers and sisters to spend significant time in a safe, healing
environment. There they can be stabilized physically, learn about
the nature of our illness, and receive therapy to heal emotionally,
including addressing mental health issues such as depression and
anxiety that create barriers to treating their addictions.

Twelve Step programs offer the third essential component for
achieving long-term recovery—a pathway to the solution that sta-
bilizes our emotional and spiritual health, which is essential for
maintaining long-term abstinence.

Dr. Silkworth believed that treatment for alcohol addiction
requires both a medical response to stabilize the patient and restore
him to physical health, and a "moral psychological" approach that
would produce an "essential psychic change." This essential psychic
change, he believed, was a curative experience that, when main-
tained, would produce a remission. Through his work with Bill W.
and other alcoholics at Towns Hospital, Silkworth came to believe
that some type of spiritual experience is absolutely essential in
order to permanently recover from alcoholism.

Now, more than ever, if Twelve Step recovery is to remain relevant throughout the twenty-first century, there is an urgent need
for Step Twelve warriors to create new tools and pathways to powerfully carry the message of our spiritual solution and offer hope,
help, and healing for those who have not yet been reached.

BILL W.'S LEGACY OF INNOVATION

I have no doubt whatsoever that if Bill W. were alive today, after his
morning guidance meditation, he would be tweeting, posting on
Facebook, and ever exploring new ways to carry the message, going
to any lengths to help another alcoholic to achieve sobriety. Bill was
prophetic and passionately believed that we needed to harness the
power of the press in order to carry our message around the globe

to everyone who needed our help. In his words, "nothing matters more to AA's future welfare than the manner in which we use the colossus of modern communication. Used unselfishly and well, it can produce results surpassing our present imagination." (Bill W., November 1960)

To that end, the National Council on Alcoholism and Drug Dependence, Inc. (NCADD), founded by Marty Mann, was tasked with the mission of actively promoting AA, Al-Anon, and Twelve Step recovery in the world press; serving as an advocate for Twelve Step recovery in mass media; and ensuring that we can reach as many people as possible.

Bill W. spoke clearly and emphatically about our need to maintain great friendships with members of mass media and giants of modern communications technology to help us carry out our Twelfth Step work to levels of maximum service.

> While word of mouth and personal contact have brought in many a newcomer, we can never forget that most of us are able to trace our chance for recovery back to our friends in communications—we read, or maybe we heard, or we saw. That is why AA now has 200,000 active members. . . .
>
> These, and a host of other experiences with the men and women of press, radio, and television, plainly tell us of what their dedication has meant. In nearly every city where AA grows today, we see our friends in communications following in the footsteps of Jack Alexander [who wrote the 1941 *Saturday Evening Post* article] and Fulton Oursler [the editor of *Liberty* magazine who printed Morris Markey's article "Alcoholics and God" in 1939]. For all such couriers of goodwill, let us be everlastingly grateful. And let us always be worthy of their friendship. (Bill W., October 1957)

It was over a decade ago that I first learned the alarming fact that over two million people die from alcohol on planet Earth each year and that the number of deaths from alcohol was rising exponentially at an alarming rate. These facts showing that our disease continued to be a plague out of control crystallized in my heart, mind, and spirit when, that same year, I learned that membership in our fellowship had been on the decline since the 1970s.

LAYING A SPIRITUAL FOUNDATION
FOR BECOMING A STEP TWELVE PIONEER

I made a vow then to dramatically expand my Step Twelve service work and carry our message to as many people as possible. At that time, some of the creative new Higher Powered tools for Twelve Step recovery education needed to pierce through the cacophony of the complex twenty-first-century society distractions that were beginning to come onto the scene. Their availability has exploded exponentially since then, which raises an important question for me: How shall we discern which new tools will be effective as we endeavor to best be of maximum service?

I wrote earlier about how our founders practiced the art of two-way prayer to receive guidance for creating the Twelve Steps, writing the Big Book, and learning new tools for working with others. Following the divine guidance they received enabled them to achieve recovery rates far higher than any we see today. By listening each morning and following their Higher Power's guidance, they entered into the fourth dimension and a vital working relationship with the God of their understanding.

For those of us who are preparing to embark on our Twelfth Step calling, if we desire to find new ways to carry our message that will be vital and relevant in the complicated societal miasma of the twenty-first century, it is imperative that we ask our Higher Power for guidance during our daily Eleventh Step meditation, asking to be shown dynamic new ways to be of maximum service to other addicts and alcoholics, and then manifest our guidance through walking the talk with Step Twelve.

On my Step Twelve journey in various programs of recovery, two-way prayer has led me to discover many new tools for carrying the message that utilize venues of mass communication and public outreach beyond the rooms of recovery and technologies unique to our times.

For decades, AA World Services and NCADD have been advocating for Twelve Step recovery by utilizing the colossus of television and radio broadcast to carry out their service work by producing highly effective commercials, which carry a simple message: if you have a problem with drugs and alcohol, go to a Twelve Step meeting—it works. I have been fortunate to be invited to serve as a frequent guest on a number of television and radio recovery talk programs. After sharing my story over the airwaves, I am always amazed when the phone lines light up with calls from hundreds of listeners reaching out for help after hearing the message, often while driving in their cars on their way to a pub, and instead make the decision to bust a U-turn and drive as fast as they can to the nearest Twelve Step meeting.

We can learn a great deal of accurate and current information regarding AA's public relations policies and how to promote Twelve Step recovery in mass media while maintaining "personal anonymity at the level of press, radio, and films" (and to that we can add the Internet), as prescribed in the Eleventh Tradition, by visiting www .aa.org. AA World Services always encourages us to work effectively with the media, with the primary goal of ensuring that active alcoholics are able to hear how we stop drinking and then learn about the effective long-term solution AA has to offer.

Though anonymity is the spiritual foundation of our Twelve Traditions, we are always encouraged to talk openly in mass media about the effectiveness of Twelve Step recovery, so long as we share only that we are recovering and that Twelve Step recovery works, and do not state that we are members of a specific Twelve Step fellowship.

TWELFTH STEPPING IN THE TWENTY-FIRST CENTURY

During preparation for this book, I had the honor of interviewing dozens of twenty-first-century Step Twelve pioneers who have followed the guidance of AA and their Higher Power, and forged astonishing new ways to carry our message using the vast resources that digital technology and mass media offer. What follows are some of the tools that I have found to be most useful and inspirational.

A Twelve Step tool that has helped me discern my Step Twelve call to action is the website created by our friend Father Bill, www .TwoWayPrayer.org, dedicated to helping members of Twelve Step fellowships deepen their experience of their Higher Power through the practice of two-way prayer. This marvelous website lays out all the information needed to begin practicing the lost art of using the Eleventh Step for daily guidance, as prescribed and practiced by our founders.

Recovery Internet Radio has become a powerful force for carrying the message. Many Recovery Radio programs, such as *Steppin' Out Radio, Addiction Recovery Radio, Rockers in Recovery Radio, Recovery Radio Network, Recovery 101, Recovery—Coast to Coast,* and *Recovery Radio Raw,* hosted by our friend Indian Bob, broadcast not only on live radio, but also through Internet platforms and podcasts.

Mike F. operates www.RecoverySpeakers.com, which archives the world's largest collection of recovery speaker talks from AA, Al-Anon, Co-Dependents Anonymous, Gamblers Anonymous, Overeaters Anonymous, Narcotics Anonymous, and Cocaine Anonymous, among others. All of these talks are downloadable and free, presenting a remarkable resource for carrying the message and Step Twelve service work.

Recovery media pioneer Leonard B. publishes the "Addiction/ Recovery eBulletin," which is disseminated through mass email to over twenty-five thousand readers each week. Leonard also produces the REEL Recovery Film Festival in cities across North America, which has catapulted documentary and feature filmmaking with recovery-based content into the mainstream cinematic consciousness.

Recovery-based Internet blogs and e-magazines, such as *The Fix, Guinevere Gets Sober, Recovery 2.0,* and *The Sober World,* reach hundreds of thousands of readers with articles bearing witness to the healing power of Twelve Step recovery.

Nearly every Twelve Step fellowship known to humans now has meetings online through Internet instant messaging chat rooms and Skyped meetings. I personally belong to over four hundred recovery-based Facebook sites with a total membership of over one million globally and often attend Twelve Step meetings online while travelling. Here's an example of how these tools are working miracles.

• • •

Recently I was asked to travel from my home in South Florida to New York City to share my recovery story at a treatment facility and then travel to carry the message in two more cities in rapid succession. My schedule was jammed up tight, but as I hopped from airport to airport, while in the cab, I would check my iPhone for messages.

I received a message from a friend in Northern California. She had just received a Facebook instant message from a former sponsee in Southern California whose sister, currently living in a small rural community in Southwest Texas, had fallen while intoxicated. She was badly injured, was hospitalized, and at long last, was seeking help for her drinking problem. The window of opportunity was wide open. Did I know anyone who might help her? Immediately I used Facebook to instant message a friend from Texas who was visiting Florida who messaged another friend in East Texas who messaged another friend in West Texas who happened to be visiting with two women from AA at that very moment. Those women happened to live in the same community as our injured, sick, and suffering alcoholic friend, and were at that moment in the same town where our new friend was currently hospitalized. Within hours, the two women showed up to conduct a Twelfth Step call—amazing grace from cyberspace.

• • •

I found another amazing tool when I recently contacted Jordan S., an outgoing, intelligent, and athletic former frat house party animal who has now devoted his professional life to working with addicts and alcoholics in San Rafael, California. Jordan, a techno buff, shared with me a remarkable story about how his sponsorship family of young men—over one thousand strong throughout Marin County—remain closely connected through Step Twelve service via membership on a daily email thread.

• • •

It's kind of funny because when I got to the Tenth Step, my sponsor said, "Hey, Jordan, there's a bunch of sober guys here on the Twelfth Step email thread, and I'm signing you up, and there's a bunch of questions that you are going to weigh in on every day. It's like a Tenth, Eleventh, and Twelfth Step daily check-in. It's about accountability, Jordan, to make sure you don't become complacent or lazy, and too busy to work Step Twelve."

If you don't answer the daily check-in, you eventually get booted off the thread, and then you are on the hot seat with your sponsor and sponsee brothers, and that's not gonna be fun or cool.

So the questions are like a daily sober "self-check survey," and every dude on the thread can see your responses. We all know each other, so you just gotta take time to do this little check and answer these twelve questions:

- *How sober are you today? (scale of 1–12)*
- *Are things good up here in your world or not?*
- *What Step do you need to apply to whatever situation is troubling you?*
- *Did you do any Tenth Step review?*
- *Did you pray?*
- *Did you do morning meditation?*
- *Did you do readings?*
- *How's your God posture throughout the day?*
- *What have you done to carry the message today?*
- *Have you practiced all Twelve Steps throughout the day?*
- *What is going on with your amends progress?*
- *Have you had enough sleep, good food, exercise, and sober fun?*

The only way you get on this thread is your sponsor brings you when you hit the Tenth Step. There are like maybe a thousand guys on this one thread, all connected through one big sponsorship family, which has grown all across this state. This thread also helps us to identify new and urgent opportunities for service work and answer Twelfth Step calls when someone in our sponsorship family puts out the "Bat Signal." It's an awesome way to carry the message and stay connected through service.

• • •

There are dozens of apps that are being used by recovering people to stay connected and do Step Twelve work, such as AA Big Book, My Spiritual Toolkit, AA Big Book Audio, 12 Steps AA Companion, and Joe and Charlie Big Book. New recovery-related apps are being created at an astonishing rate. Most of my friends in recovery in Delray Beach, Florida, are addicted to a new phone app called Sober Grid, which I have found incredibly useful in my Step Twelve service work. This is a free iOS/Android app that connects you with other sober people. You are instantly connected to a sober community in your neighborhood and around the globe. It's a virtual sober community in the palm of your hands.

Sober Grid has become a go-to for many of my sponsees who have lost their driving privileges. They are able to use Sober Grid to find rides to meetings and sober social events. It is the sober Uber and rapidly becoming an indispensable weapon in our Step Twelve battle arsenal.

Sober Grid users, who can choose to remain anonymous, can use a GPS locator to find sober friends while travelling, in an airport, or in a new city. Users can also enter the name of another user and locate them by geographic location to help find sober friends anywhere in the world.

Sober Grid chat and messaging functions allow users to share their thoughts, experiences, struggles, and hopes associated with sobriety and addiction recovery, and also has a feature that allows users to send their location to another user if they would like to meet up. If in need, users can select the "Burning Desire" button to let other sober people know they need help. This feature also provides an opportunity for those who want to practice Step Twelve, and connect with and help others who may be having a difficult time.

There are other apps being used by growing numbers of people to stay clean and sober. There are even dating and vacation-planning apps, such as the one available at www.cleanfunnetwork .com. The mission of Clean Fun Network (CFN) is to connect those who are committed to sobriety and seek a life filled with exciting, adventurous, sober fun. Many think that when they get sober, that will be the end of fun as they know it. CFN helps newcomers in sobriety discover an exciting, fun, and fulfilling road ahead, and provides a safe, comfortable environment for dating and sober social activities and vacations.

Our friend Troy K. shared with me another remarkable app called Trigger, which is being widely used for Step Twelve service among his sober peers and fellow treatment alumni.

• • •

There is this app on my phone that is used by the treatment center that I went to. I am on it because I am active in our alumni program and a bunch of my sponsees are on it—it is called Trigger.

Basically it is a group message tool that everybody who was in treatment with me and much of my sponsorship family of sober brothers in recovery can use—but just the people who are doing the deal. If they get high, they get taken off. It allows you to maintain constant contact with your clean and sober support group; I am very active in it.

The app does a couple of different things: you create a profile about your sober life, and you put on your sober anniversary date. The app keeps track of your clean and sober time, announcing your day count, and every day it asks you questions, such as, "Have you used drugs today, yes or no?" If you click yes, it alerts the people at the treatment center and your support group. Then an email is sent out to your clean and sober network saying, "Hey, everybody, this guy is in trouble, and you should reach out to this person right now."

For me the best part of it is, at 9:00 p.m. every day, it asks you how your day was on a scale of one to ten. And the reason I wanted it was because of that feature. If you ask me how my day is going at four o'clock and how my day is going at six or seven or throughout the day, I might not rate it too highly, but at night if you ask me how my day was when I lay my head down on my pillow, if I got through the day clean and sober and helped another addict or alcoholic, then it is always a ten; no matter what happened, it is always a ten.

Another feature is that we can all put into our profile what meetings we are planning on attending, so all of our network can know where they can find us at specific times of the day if we want to connect face-to-face at a meeting.

I am also able to schedule my Step Twelve service work on this app, which helps me stay on the recovery beam 24/7. It helps me to stay orga-nized so that I can carry the message more efficiently and maximize my potential for service and stay sober, live large, and have a blast in recovery by staying in close contact with many friends in my recovery life, loving each other up every minute of the day and night. It doesn't get any better than that.

• • •

Many old-timers may say that the Twelfth Step call is dying, but as we're seeing with these new tools that are proliferating, I don't think that is entirely true. In today's rapidly changing world, every-thing looks different as our culture and technology change minute by minute. The younger generations are totally reinventing the recovery paradigm to fit into our new world. They embody "more will be revealed." They are not rigid nor are they afraid to receive new guidance. They are powerfully utilizing these wonderful new tools in their Twelve Step work.

Mike F. shared me with me an experience he had recently that typifies the old guard's fear of change and the new guard's embrac-ing of new recovery tools.

• • •

I went up to a couple of people after a meeting one day, and I was angry and read them the riot act, saying, "You know, at this meeting we are reading the Big Book, we're trying to have a meeting, and you guys are looking at your damn cell phones." They all laughed and said, "Yeah, dude—the Big Book's on the iPhone."

• • •

I believe that our young Step Twelve warriors are saving our fellowship and ushering in that which God is revealing for us to remain relevant in this new century.

THE PUBLIC FACE OF STEP TWELVE

Another major change in our time that has redefined how Step Twelve is practiced is the trend of people in entertainment coming out of addiction treatment and going public about their recovery. Many of them do it explicitly to remove the stigma of addiction and to encourage others to seek help. They share their stories of recovery openly on reality television programs, and their Fifth Step confessions and Twelfth Step calls manifest in the form of best-selling books, such as Kristen Johnston's *Guts: The Endless Follies and Tiny Triumphs of a Giant Disaster* and Mackenzie Phillips's *High on Arrival: A Memoir*.

There are musicians, such as Eminem, Machine Gun Kelly, John McAndrew, and LaVerne Tripp, who carry the message of recovery and practice Step Twelve through their music and lyrics. Through their CDs and MP3s, as well as their live and digitally recorded concerts available on YouTube and other Internet platforms, these artists are carrying the message to millions with recovery-based music moving the spiritual solution to addiction out of the shadows and into the proud light of day and mainstream popular culture.

Always ahead of his time, Robin Williams was perhaps the first internationally known comic to begin doing sets entirely devoted to his experiences with addiction and recovery. Many other comics followed suit, including Craig Ferguson and David Letterman. Today, recovery-based comedy has become a staple of American culture and available to recovery communities and the general public alike from coast to coast, thanks to the work of recovery comedians such as Jimmy Labriola, Mark Lundholm, Alonzo Bodden, Moshe Kasher, Kristee Ono, Jason Stuart, Sarge, and Mary Wilkerson who carry the message through laughter and remind us not to take ourselves too seriously. These courageous performing artists embody the concept that we are not a glum lot and heal us through spiritual principles of raw honesty and unselfishness—sharing their personal pains and triumphs with mass audiences.

Step Twelve pioneers who carry the message of hope through the power of the performing arts have accomplished what no one else had been able to do previously. They have effectively dealt a death blow to the shame and isolation of our disease by sharing about the true nature of our illness and the hope of Twelve Step recovery in public forums.

Live stage productions that carry the message of recovery are becoming a staple of our national theatrical diet. Theatrical Step Twelve vanguards have included Carrie Fisher's one-woman show, *Wishful Drinking,* and *The Darrell Hammond Project,* the stage adaptation of his recovery memoir, *God, If You're Not Up There, I'm F*cked.*

As I shared in my story, I was fortunate to be a part of this movement when I was guided to write the stage play *Pass It On . . . An Evening with Bill W. & Dr. Bob*—an ongoing touring production presented by the National Council on Alcoholism and Drug Dependence—that tells the inspirational and often hilarious true story of our beloved cofounders of AA as they stumbled onto the discovery of Twelve Step recovery in 1935.

In each city that we travel to, this play generates a dialogue about Twelve Step recovery in local media and with local government, law enforcement, educators, and the military. Through the powerful medium of live theater, we preserve the history and legacy of the Twelve Step movement, present the spiritual solution found in the Twelve Steps, demystify what happens at an AA meeting, and reach people who cannot be reached any other way.

Over the past several years, we have performed this live stage production in dozens of cities in the United States and Canada, and have reached audience members numbering in the tens of thousands.

We have received hundreds of letters, emails, and phone calls of gratitude from audience members who heard the message for the first time and began their recovery journey.

I will share one such example with you.

In 2012 the national tour of *Pass It On* opened in Ft. Myers, Florida, for a week-long engagement. The event was covered heavily in the local press on television and radio and in print media. A local college professor whose husband and son—both prominent doctors, a psychiatrist and a surgeon—were falling-down drunks in late stages of untreated alcoholism, had read about our production in the newspaper and, since she had long ago been forbidden to lecture her husband and son about their drinking, saw this as an opportunity to do a second-hand intervention. All three members of this highly educated family were avid theatergoers. She told her husband and son that a touring production of a new comedy about a drunken rectal surgeon and stockbroker was coming to Ft. Myers. They said it sounded funny and encouraged her to reserve tickets—they had no idea that they were about to attend a theatrical performance that carried the message of Twelve Step recovery.

I well remember these two men who were hammered when they arrived at the theater and sat in the front row, right in front of me, as I stood on stage at the beginning of the performance portraying the role of Bill W. Following my opening line, "My name is Bill W. and I am an alcoholic," both men, in thick, boozy, slurred speech, laughed and shouted, "Hey, Bill, here's to ya! Cheers! Skoal!" and so forth.

During intermission, they were pounding down the coffee. All during the second act, as we presented the spiritual solution to our deadly disease, both men sat with tears streaming down their faces.

Here were two doctors who were not previously able to comprehend and understand that they have a disease. At the end of the performance, the son leaned over to the father and said, "Dad, I never really understood that we have a disease. We are very ill and need to go to AA." The next morning they both went to their first AA meeting and our college professor went to her first Al-Anon meeting.

Several months later, we received a beautiful email from this wonderful family on the road to recovery. One year later, we returned to Ft. Myers with a reengagement of our production, and we presented the two men with their first-year sobriety medallions from the stage following the performance.

God, in his infinite wisdom and mercy, has revealed astonishing new ways to reach record numbers of addicts and alcoholics, and plant the first seeds of hope.

If our way of life and our Twelve Step programs are to survive and flourish into the next century, we are going to have to make dramatic adjustments and recommit to rolling up our sleeves and walking the talk with Step Twelve.

TWELFTH STEPPING REHAB AND OTHER INSTITUTIONAL SETTINGS

Some old-timers say that it was with the growth of the addiction treatment industry that the AA program became marginalized and the art of the Twelfth Step began to be lost. I believe that, just as we have discovered dazzling new ways to carry our message to mass audiences through technology, we also need to find new creative ways to work with treatment centers in order to reach their patients one-on-one within the first days of their recovery when they are most teachable—when they are willing and able to hear our message about the spiritual solution to our common disease and before the window of opportunity closes.

In many cases, to work as a sponsor with new clients in a treatment facility, it is now a requirement to become a certified recovery coach in order to gain access to the patient in treatment and be in compliance with privacy and health industry regulations. So be it. In those cases, we must become recovery coaches before we become sponsors, develop intimate friendly relationships with treatment centers, and get to their clients as quickly as possible, while they are still desperate and teachable.

In a *Grapevine* article from October 1965, Bill W. emphatically detailed his views regarding the need for close partnership with all who endeavor to heal those afflicted with our common disease, including those in the business of addiction research, education, and rehabilitation:

> We should very seriously ask ourselves how many alcoholics have gone on drinking simply because we have failed to cooperate in good spirit with these many agencies. No alcoholic should go mad or die merely because he did not come straight to AA in the beginning.

In Delray Beach, Florida, our local intergroup is pioneering a new Step Twelve service commitment called Bridging the Gap Twelfth Step service. Members can sign up at intergroup to be on call for sponsorship and mentoring. Through Bridging the Gap, we make a Step Twelve service commitment to show up at the door of the treatment facility, detox, or prison on the day of discharge to personally take the hand of newcomers and accompany them to meetings, arrange for rides, introduce them to sponsors, become their sponsors, take them through the Steps, and usher them into our fellowship and way of life. We sign up as a community to sponsor them collectively—whether fresh from the bar, the shooting gallery, the treatment center, or the prison, we will tag team shadow them until they gel. It is imperative that we get to them any way we can—not only for their survival, but also for the survival of our Twelve Step fellowships and way of life.

We can no longer sit in our church basements saying, "let them come and find us," as we cluck our tongues and chant "attraction not promotion,"—the catchphrase many hide behind to avoid walking their talk with Step Twelve.

It's a brave new world, and we must be flexible, teachable, and courageous in order to fulfill our mandate to be of maximum service.

While technology and mass communications have given us a glorious opportunity to reach more fellow sufferers than ever, today membership in many Twelve Step fellowships appears to be on the decline, and in many locations AA is an aging population. A number of trusted servants who currently serve as general service representatives and work directly with World Services shared with me that, according to the General Service Office, less than 50 percent of our members currently study the Big Book, work all twelve Steps, and sponsor others, which has resulted in a decline in membership and our success rate.

However, a new generation of addicts are coming into recovery cross-addicted to multiple substances and are finding the support they need in other Twelve Step fellowships, such as Narcotics Anonymous, Heroin Anonymous, Marijuana Anonymous, and Cocaine Anonymous.

As for AA, any organization that is not growing is dying. No matter how many millions we can reach through the marvels of modern communication technologies, once they show up in the rooms, we still have to move a muscle, put on a pot of coffee, sponsor them, and take them through the Steps so that they begin to live a life of service and stick around.

It is through living in Step Twelve that we come to realize with certainty that alcohol and other drugs are just symptoms of our problem, that what we are truly suffering from is spiritual disconnection and that, through fear, laziness, and selfishness, we had become separated from our spiritual source.

We learned to trust our Higher Power during our journey through the first eleven Steps. Let's trust the God of our understanding to guide us and take care of us through our ongoing Twelfth Step service work.

PART IV

Testimonials—The Twelfth Step Call in Action

⁂

Embarking on a Twelfth Step call is an act of faith, a spiritual discipline. During a Twelfth Step call, we are asked to step out of our comfort zone, face our fears, and venture into the unknown in service to the God of our understanding and our fellows. Twelfth Step calls are often hard work and can sometimes be unnerving and disconcerting—that goes with the territory.

If we allow ourselves to continue trusting that our Higher Power will care for us as we sally forth on our Twelfth Step calls, our fears, our sloth, and our self-doubts will disappear, ensuring our ability to be effective and ever-willing to fulfill our Twelfth Step mandate to be of maximum service.

Rarely will our Twelfth Step calls unfold according to our will, as we had planned. We follow suggested guidelines to the best of our ability and let go of the outcomes. We are merely humble servants carrying our simple message of hope and help. Our Higher Power does the healing. We simply prime the pump.

Remember: ultimately there is no perfect or right or wrong way to conduct the Twelfth Step call. Each call will be unique and unfold organically. Many of my Twelfth Step calls that I perceived as having gone off the rails ended up saving a life.

Presented here are testimonials I have gathered from Step Twelve warriors who exemplify Step Twelve in action. They have achieved quality ongoing sobriety and live remarkable lives as a direct result of their prodigious Twelfth Step service work. None of them have done their Twelfth Step calls perfectly. The gifts that they received as a result of their willingness to come out of their comfort zones and march out into the fray in service to the greater good are the sweetest fruits that life has to offer. The lessons learned from their Twelfth Step call adventures and misadventures are priceless.

Easy Does It

❧

I learned what a Twelfth Step call was when I had my first encounter with AA in October of 1948. I was twenty-three years old. Twelfth Step calls were always very personal back then—people called on you at your home. I was living out in California, and I wrote a letter to AA and said I needed help with my drinking and asked what I would have to do to join their outfit. A few days later, I got a phone call at the rooming house I was staying in, and the next thing I know, this guy picked me up in his car and took me for a visit with a few of his friends at their house. They happened to be people, from Akron Group No. 1, who had gotten sober a few years earlier.

They had a bunch of guys in their living room, and they asked me a bunch of questions, told me what had happened to them, and then talked to me all about the Steps and how this deal works. Then they asked me if I wanted it. It all sounded pretty good to me, and I said sure, I'd like to join. This Twelfth Step call took about an hour or so, and I was sold—so off we all went and they took me to my first meeting.

At the meetings, those fellas showed me what to do and it was all pretty simple—of course, I really wanted it. Things got better right away, although I did pick up a drink a few times after that while I learned how to practice these principles in my life. We didn't work formal Steps in those days—at least we didn't do any writing. We just talked about the Steps and made amends and changed our behavior. It was all about action, and it was pretty simple. Once I finally got it, I kept going to meetings, doing service, telling my story, asking God for guidance, and practicing the Steps continuously every day of my life, and that has kept me sober since 1950. It's given me a pretty good life. Service to others and God in our lives is what makes this thing work—and stories. AA is stories—we tell our stories; that's how we come together and find God through our stories.

Mel B. *is a prominent AA historian and was an editor of the* AA Grape-vine *and coauthor of Bill W.'s official biography,* Pass It On. *Mel was a close friend of Bill W. and Lois. As of this writing, he has been sober for sixty-six years.*

He Answered the Call

It was 1987. I was eighteen months sober. I thought that I wanted to be an attorney. I went to law school and six weeks in, I said to myself, "I don't want to be a lawyer."

I was sober enough at the time and working Steps, and I said to God "Okay, if you close one door, another will open." I couldn't stop wondering about what I was going to do, and I needed to get out of my head, so I went to an AA meeting.

So I was at this meeting, wondering what God has in store for me. The room was packed and I was standing up in the back, propped up against the back wall of the clubhouse, and every time I went to a meeting, I always looked for newcomers to welcome. I spotted this guy who is obviously deaf—the person sitting next to him was doing her best at mouthing what was going on in the meeting.

I kept on looking at this guy and I was saying in my head, how is this guy ever going to get the message that is so critical to my life and so critical to saving his life? How is this supposed to happen for him?

It was at this moment, literally at this moment, that the entire trajectory of my life changed. I did not know how to communicate with this guy—I don't know sign language—and I couldn't stop looking at this guy and I was thinking, God, do I leave this problem to somebody else or do I introduce myself to this newcomer like I normally would do?

I worked Step Three and turned it over, then I worked Step Eleven and asked for guidance and listened; then I worked Step Twelve and took action, walked through my fear, and made the choice to introduce myself to this guy.

After that icebreaker, my fear vanished. I stopped thinking about myself and just focused on helping this deaf guy get the message. Next thing you know, I was dragging him around to meetings, writing on a pad, knowing full well that English was not his first language. Before I knew it, I was taking a class and learning sign language myself.

My deaf sponsee told his friends about me, and the next thing you know, I had five or six deaf guys showing up at the recovery club in Trenton and asking everyone where "sign language John" is.

I laugh today because God, of course, knew that I was impatient in my early sobriety, and He also knew that I was eager and willing to do whatever it takes to work Step Twelve and remain sober, so within two weeks I got my calling to work with deaf alcoholics. From the point that I surrendered to that Twelfth Step service call and came out of my comfort zone, my whole professional life rocketed into the fourth dimension and changed beyond my comprehension.

Very shortly thereafter, I was given the divine idea to found an agency for deaf alcoholics called Signs of Sobriety, which provided a service to the deaf recovering population, helping carry the message of God's spiritual solution to alcoholism and addiction. Literally thousands of other disabled and deaf individuals in my state have been helped because of that first meeting when I reached out to my new deaf friend. To this day, when the shit hits the fan and I am still trying to figure out what I want to do when I grow up, I find somebody to help through Twelfth Step service work. That is where the great power of our society is found.

Through doing service work with deaf alcoholics, I met the mother of my children, my lovely wife, who is deaf. Imagine how profound that is for me to know that in that single moment in time, by making that choice to walk through my fear, my whole life changed.

John H. *has been sober for thirty years as of this writing. His work at Signs of Sobriety led him to a position with the National Council on Alcoholism and Drug Dependence in New Jersey, conducting govern-*

ment relations and policy work for sixteen years, which in turn led him to work as a policy advisor in the governor's office, resulting in John being appointed as the state drug czar.

Willing to Go to Any Lengths

❦

There was this guy who was living in absolute abject poverty, and he called the central office and asked for help. I grabbed a buddy from the rooms, and we went out on the Twelfth Step call to carry the message to him. This guy was literally knocking on death's door. He sat there and drank through the whole call, while we talked and talked about the spiritual solution and told him our stories. He passed out in his chair, dead to the world. We couldn't wake him up or get him out of the chair, so we picked him up, still in his chair, and we put him in the back of our flatbed pickup truck. We used ratchet straps and strapped him into the chair, strapped the chair onto the truck, and drove him all the way across Michigan. We dropped him off in his chair at a detox where we had made arrangements for him to check in. He never woke up the entire trip.

This was all seriously comical at the time, and we never laughed so hard that entire drive. I will never forget it—one of the high points of my sobriety. I worked with the guy for four years after that as a sponsor. At one point he stopped coming around, and he went out and started drinking. He never spun out of it and he died—but working with him kept me sober. I wouldn't trade that Twelfth Step call for the world.

Mike H. *chronically relapsed for many years until he finally embraced all Twelve Steps. During that time, thankfully, no one gave up on him. Today he is sober in long-term recovery and has become a dynamic addictions counselor and founder of Randy's House in Grand Rapids, Michigan, which provides lifesaving recovery services to men in need of support. Mike is a tireless Twelve Step soldier, always willing to go to any length to help someone in trouble, and is never afraid to take a risk if it might help a drunk or junkie. His Twelfth Step calls are the stuff of legend in the rooms, and he never gives up on anyone.*

He Had a Sober Purpose
for Being There

I started going on Twelfth Step calls almost immediately. We had a really large recovery club in Dallas; we were upstairs over a well-known dance studio, so there was always a lot of noise and a lot of traffic, and everybody knew about this club. We had a full-time secretary who was a member and people called there often, desperate to be helped. I used to hang around there and when a call came in, I went.

I learned a few things right off the bat, such as I don't give advice anymore; I just talk about my experience. When I was about five or six months sober, I made the biggest mistake and went out on a Twelfth Step call by myself, even though I knew I was never to do that—my sponsor had warned me, but there was nobody to come with me, and I wasn't about to just turn my back on the call.

I went to this guy's apartment and I talked to him for about maybe an hour. He was drinking the whole time—there had been nothing untoward going on, there were no threats or anything like that—but by the time I got up to leave and got into my car, I wanted to drink worse than I have wanted to drink in my life. I have never been able to fully understand that experience or why that was, but it was a dangerous time, when you're around illness like that. Not only had I gone alone, but I also had forgotten to pray.

Two valuable lessons: say a prayer and take along another AA. Having said that, there are exceptions to every rule, which are actually only suggestions after all.

On one other occasion, I conducted a Twelfth Step call alone again, but on this occasion, I remembered to call on God before trying to do his work. While driving around town, I spotted a drunken bum under a bridge and I actually picked him up. I got him in the car, and I was going to take him to a meeting. He was already pretty sideways and he told me that he was a dentist, which was hard to believe—this guy looked pretty shot out and grimy and weather-beaten.

Instead of taking him to a meeting, I felt compelled to take him to the detox at the VA hospital. Normally they would have turned him out, but they admitted him right away. Turns out he really was a dentist. I spent some time sharing my story, talking about how we work a simple program with a spiritual solution, and told him how it worked for me. I kept it all very friendly and then I left him there. I went back a few days later to check on him, but he had been discharged and I lost track of him.

I showed up to a speaker meeting about three years later, and there he was—sober, sharing his story, passing it on to others. He was working as a dentist again, and you know, coming from a guy who was living under a bridge on the Trinity River, that's a long way up. That was just the greatest feeling, seeing that man sober and alive and awake and vital. Twelfth Step work is something you don't want to miss out on. There's nothing in the world like it.

Bob G. *got sober in 1983, changed careers, and began working in the field of addiction treatment while conducting Twelfth Step calls on the mean streets of Las Vegas, the drinking capital of the world. Bob is a living example of our ability to safely do our work, even in the presence of liquor. So long as we are spiritually fit, there is nothing to fear.*

She Laid Out a Spiritual Tool Kit

⟨❊⟩

There is a weekly Twelfth Step service call that I do that probably means more to me than almost anything else I do for my sobriety or anything else I do in my life.

When it was time for me to do my Ninth Step amends, I was a blackout drinker and a thief, so I can't always make amends, because there were a whole lot of people that I have stolen from—some were strangers and some were businesses.

So my sponsor suggested that I find a way to make societal amends, and she strongly suggested, since I never went to jail or prison, that I find a way to help women who are incarcerated, which is what I should have been.

There happened to be a gentleman coming to speak at a church in our neighborhood who was a warden of a minimum security prison near us, about the time that my sponsor was talking to me about societal amends. So I went to listen to this warden speak and found out that the prison is about three miles from my house, and I had no clue that it was there.

He said, "I am going to throw some numbers at you, and the numbers are three, seven, and sixteen. Right now I have three inmates that have children with seven different women. That is sixteen children that do not have their daddy right now, and, because these inmates are chemically dependent, if we can help their addiction, the kids can have their daddy back." That was really profoundly inspirational for me.

In this particular prison, every single inmate has committed a crime while under the influence of drugs or alcohol, so they get treatment while they are in this facility. It is a nine-month boot camp–style program.

About a year after I heard this gentleman speak, they began to take women into this program. I made a proposal to the warden offering to do Twelfth Step calls with the women, and because I had never been incarcerated, I was able to pass the background checks and my offer was accepted.

Now I take women from this facility outside the prison, without a guard, three at a time, to their very first AA meeting outside the walls. I have been granted permission to do this twice a week during the last four weeks of their incarceration.

So I get to know them, and I get to carry our message about the spiritual solution that will release them from the bondage of addiction and set them free. I have been doing that for about twelve years, twice a week.

Truthfully, they have taught me more about freedom than I could ever teach.

Jody K. *is a tireless Twelve Step missionary, sober since 1983. If you attend any major AA functions around the nation, it's likely you have met her. She lives and breathes Step Twelve in every aspect of her life and embodies the concept that no personal sacrifice of time and energy is too great for the preservation of the fellowship.*

He Pocketed His Pride

Years ago I got a call from a guy who was in bad shape. I knew it was a Twelfth Step call and I went by myself—I made the decision to rely on the strength and guidance of my Higher Power, whom I choose to call "Honey."

So I went to the house of this sick drunk who called for help, and when he came to his door, he was wearing some of the worst drag I had ever seen and he was wasted. I don't know for sure what he wanted me to do—maybe he wanted me to say that it was ok that he was dressed up like a girl. I don't know if he was straight or gay, and it didn't matter. What mattered was that he was a sick alcoholic and wanted to get sober. I tried to share about the program and what had worked for me, but I found it extremely difficult to focus at times because I was driven to distraction by the awful drag outfit he had on, which for some reason made it impossible for me to talk about the spiritual solution.

By the way, that guy did get sober and apparently had a spiritual awakening—and his drag has improved immeasurably in sobriety!

John S., *sober since 1991, was an integral part of my early recovery. He personifies the slogan "we are not a glum lot." John was the first person to make me laugh in sobriety at my very first AA meeting after being discharged from my first treatment center experience. John was also the first person to carry the message of Debtors Anonymous and Al-Anon to me. For many years, John has given his time freely in service to several Twelve Step programs, including AA, Debtors Anonymous, Overeaters Anonymous, and Al-Anon.*

She Spoke the Language
of the Heart

The more I practiced the Twelfth Step call, it seemed that God would increase the level of complexity of each call that I went on. I felt as if I had been promoted to a new level of service work when I was trusted with the opportunity to conduct an old-school-style Twelfth Step call right out of the Big Book.

A good friend of mine started attending my women's Monday night meetings. She just could not digest Alcoholics Anonymous the way that some of us are blessed to get the message quickly. She kept going back out and back out, and I would reach out to her the way we do in AA and say, "I am here for you. Let's make a meeting together sometime, or let's grab coffee and talk sometime. Maybe I could help you exercise the parts of the program that you are stumbling over and keeping you in active addiction." I was gentle, but I was persistent.

One night I got a frantic phone call from her, and she was just annihilated, I mean, super hammered, and she said, "I need help, I need help, I've had it! This is it!" So I called a couple sobriety sisters—I realized that it was going to take an army to do this Twelfth Step call. In an important situation, you go quickly so you don't miss your chance and you do not go alone, which increases your ability to get the message out clearly no matter what circumstances may be present. I was taught that you make sure that you have other people that have worked the Twelve Steps, at least one person who has had significant time in recovery, and I always try to have someone along on the call who does not have so much time, so they can be on the front line to learn and see what it is like.

So I went over to her place, and her father was there. He was a Vietnamese gentleman, and he could hardly speak English. We got her into her room away from her father, and we assessed the situation. Inside the house, there were two girls dealing with her drama, sharing their stories, talking about solutions. I was sure she couldn't hear it at this point, but she seemed comforted and was getting a lot of love and had a small group of spiritually empowered sober women loving her up and surrounding her now.

I was sitting outside with her father reading from the Big Book, "The Family Afterward," to this man who is Vietnamese, slowly breaking it down, patiently dissecting it for him, trying to explain to this man with a language barrier what's going on and why his daughter is the way that she is. He started to understand in spite of the language barrier because I am speaking the language of the heart.

It was powerful: the other girls were with his daughter inside talking about how they had found a solution through the Twelve Steps, while I was explaining to her frightened father about what is going on with her.

He sees it as, "This girl is bad . . . my daughter is a nightmare, what is wrong with her? What is wrong with her?" So I was given a precious opportunity to share with him that his daughter has a disease and that she is not a degenerate. She is ill and in need of a treatment, and we have a solution. I was able to help him understand that the solution worked for all of the women who were there to help his daughter. After a very long time, he began to comprehend and trust us, and he calmed down and found some relief.

We got her into detox and visited her every day—all of us, this entire group of sober women—and then we brought her to meetings and brought her through the Steps. We didn't let her out of our sight until she was stable and had experienced her own awakening. She is sober now and carries the message of recovery to other women through her own service commitments; to be a part of that—to watch that happen—there are really no words to describe the experience and what we get from that.

Ali H., *sober since 2009, fights on the front lines of the battle against addiction and alcoholism in Laguna Beach, California. Ali is a true Step Twelve warrior, always committed to doing anything she can to be helpful to another alcoholic who is in need of healing.*

He Did Not Hesitate

❧

I saw this guy at a meeting, and he was really struggling. He was drunk and high—I think he was doing crystal meth—and I was like, "listen, we got to get you some help." He also had some health problems, and I was going to help him get into detox, and he was like, "I am not done." So I said, "Well, go and drink and use as much drugs as you can, and then call me."

So he called me about a week later, and he was in this Motel 6 with a friend who also wanted help. I knew the other guy who was with him—he was a drug dealer who had been helped to get sober and then he went back out.

So I went into the motel with my Twelfth Step buddy, and the first thing that happened was I saw the other guy running to his truck because he saw us coming—we figured that he had changed his mind about getting sober. So we went into the little motel room and the guy who phoned me was in the room with all this stereo equipment. It was like this tiny room with all this stolen stuff. And there were drugs and booze everywhere, and I said, "Oh my God."

We got all the booze and drugs and flushed them and got him into our car, and we were able to get him into treatment, but the Twelfth Step call didn't end there. We decided that we needed to find the other guy and work on him next. We were on a roll.

So we drove all around the area, and he finally turned up on the street. He had ditched that truck, and he saw us and jumped the fence at the sleazy Regency Hotel, which is a cash, pay-by-the-hour hangout for drug addicts.

So we pulled up to the hotel, and there was a pimp, a drug dealer, and some other very hard, dangerous characters hanging out in front. I was wearing khakis and a brightly colored flowered shirt, and I got out of the car and they gave me a lot of grief, and I said, "Listen dudes, I am from AA and I am trying to help Steve." And they were like, "Oh. Wow. Holy shit. OK. OK." So me, my Twelfth Step buddy, the pimp, the drug dealer, and the gangbangers turn into a search party. Even they knew that this guy Steve was going to die if he didn't get help soon, so they were all in about helping us track him down.

These guys were armed to the teeth, and we went searching through the hotel, room by room—two AAs, the pimp, the drug dealer, and the gangbangers, all looking for this guy so that we could conduct our Twelfth Step call. We eventually found him, Twelfth Stepped his ass, and got him into a detox that was located nearby, right there on the beach.

He got sober, and today is one of my best friends in the world and has saved countless lives through his Twelfth Step work.

David A. *has carried our lifesaving message to hundreds of young people throughout Southern California. He has served as the tip of the spear in starting up numerous Back to Basics beginners meetings designed to take newcomers through the Steps quickly.*

Action Is the Key Word

⚜

Today I get high from doing Twelfth Step calls. I was clean and sober and had worked the first eleven Steps, and yet I was still miserable, restless, irritable, and discontent. I tried moving, getting a new girlfriend, a new job, and nothing made me feel better.

Relief finally came the day that I began working Step Twelve by giving of my time—intensively working with others through Twelfth Step call service and sponsorship, which is what brought my spiritual awakening.

I had this one guy who was in real trouble with drugs and alcohol, and he was nineteen also, just like me, and so he had a very special place in my heart. To work with another guy, somebody my age, is something special to me. I get to see myself in him, and I don't know why, but he just couldn't get sober—he just seemed incapable of being honest with himself, but I didn't want to give up on him.

One night he calls me up and he is like, "Dude, I did it again, I got high," and I was like, "Okay, buddy, we got you," and he was like, "I am so sorry, are you going to give up on me?" and I was like, "No, dude, why would I do that? I don't care what you did. I care about what you are going to do next, what you are doing now to get well." He said, "I am at this halfway house, and I am so depressed," and I said, "You just sit tight—we are on our way."

I called one of my buddies and said, "What are you doing tonight, dude? Hope you're not busy—we got a guy in trouble. Let's do it! We gotta scoop him up and take him to a meeting."

Of course I never go alone, and I never have to go alone because we have this awesome sponsorship family—it's huge and, because in our sponsorship family service is the number one priority, we all do service like crazy and we all have 24/7 access to all these really great guys. So when I need somebody to go with me on a Twelfth Step call, it does not even matter how late it is as I will hear back from all of them; they are all awake or they will wake up and call me back.

I have this enormous list of names of guys in my sober family in my iPhone contact list, so I put the word out that we have a sick guy going down hard who needs our help. I didn't even know which ones I called, and within a half hour we were five deep in this little PT Cruiser, and we showed up at his door. He was just so shot and high and in a really dark place. All of us sober dudes were laughing and having a good time while we worked with him, and then we saw that he had a little smile.

We put some food in his belly, and we kept laughing and talking and enjoying the camaraderie, and he flashed another smile, and we put a little coffee in him, and eventually he started to laugh. So now we knew he was ready to receive the message, and we took him to a sunrise meeting. By the end of the meeting, he was laughing again, he was crying again, and you know, he was feeling again. His emotions were back, and he was himself again. And that is recovery, Steps One, Two, and Three, all at one time. He did Steps One, Two, and Three at least four more times like that, and one of these days—who knows when—if he doesn't die, he will eventually get it. And between now and then, whenever he calls, I will be there for him.

At the age of nineteen, **Troy K.** *has been on hundreds of Twelfth Step calls. He does so much service work that he needs to have his day planner with him 24/7.*

She Didn't Want What We Have

⚜

A couple of years ago, we had a girl that called us up, a neighbor of mine, desperate for help. I didn't know her that well. She drank a lot and I was sober, so we didn't mix. So I called up my Twelve Step partner Jane—she was driving—and we showed up at this gal's home. She was really sick, and we thought she needed to be hospitalized. She had a fussy little dog with her, and she was all worried about the dog and said that the dog had to be taken care of before she could get sober. She had all of the dog's papers and she had her own papers and everything was very organized—you could tell she had really put a lot of thought into this. It appeared that she had made the decision that she was going to go off and get well and do whatever it takes.

Everything was all packed and we had her little dog in a cage and she is all ready to go to the hospital, but first she insisted that we take her dog to this fancy kennel. She was in such bad shape that she could not even sign the dog into the kennel. We had to help her hold the pen and moved the paper around under her hand so she could make her mark. She had the shakes real bad. We figured she was about to have a seizure.

Jane and I looked at each other, and we decided that we had better not do this on our own, so we called EMS.

So the ambulance arrived and the EMS gals asked us "Who are you?" and we said that we were just friends and when we said, "We don't want to go with her, so please just take her," one of the gals kind of cocked her head and squinted and smiled a little and whispered, "Are you AA?" We said yes, and she said, "Okay, I understand. That is fine. Thank you for your service," and she kind of winked at us and of course no more questions were asked.

We told the sick gal that when she gets out of the hospital she ought to come and join us at AA. She declared emphatically that AA wouldn't be necessary: "No, no, no. The doctor said that if I ever drink again I am going to die, so why would I drink again—that would be insane." So I said, "Why don't you join us anyway? I mean you'd make a lot of friends, we have a lot of fun, you would have a lot of support, and we would help you stay sober. After all, this is a life-and-death errand we are on—this thing is no joke. Why not join us anyway, what have you got to lose?" She insisted again that she was never going to drink, and I got the signal loud and clear so I did not argue with her further. We wished her well and we went home. Jane and I both knew from years of experience that her unwillingness to let us help was no reflection on our ability to carry the message.

We kept tabs on her. She got out of the hospital, and six months later she drank and she died.

Some just don't want what we have, but you try to help anyway. That's just what we do. To do nothing would be just selfish beyond belief, after so many people helped us get sober.

Over the years, I've done hundreds of Twelfth Step calls. Some are victories, and some are discouraging and even heartbreaking, and believe me when I tell you, that kind of face-to-face foxhole service work will really keep you sober.

That kind of Twelfth Step service work is what keeps us from dying before our time—and I should know: I am ninety-eight, and I have been taking Twelfth Step calls, sponsoring women, and sharing my story at meetings since 1953!

Mary B. *is a fearless Twelfth Step service warrior who is never discouraged if her prospect does not respond. Mary's Step Twelve metal was burnished in the spiritual furnace of early AA in Cleveland, where she started some of the first women's meetings in history. In her nineties, she continued to sail her yacht, flying the AA symbol on the masthead in order to instigate impromptu meetings in exotic ports of call where she carries our message to mariners, sailors, and fellow adventurers who are in need of and want what she has.*

As a result of the Twelfth Step service calls conducted as she carried the message to her family members, she has sobered up her children, grandchildren, great-grandchildren and great-great-grandchildren— creating a sober dynasty of AAs.

Call to Action

❦

Each of the men and women whose stories you just read have few things in common except they were all willing to go to any lengths to pass it on in order to maintain their long-term sobriety.

In sometimes less-than-perfect circumstances and with various levels of expertise, they never gave up or allowed fear, sloth, or self-doubt to divert them from their primary purpose. They were always willing to walk the talk with Step Twelve.

Our statement of purpose, "When anyone, anywhere, reaches out for help, I want the hand of AA always to be there. And for that I am responsible" is more than a bumper sticker or a nifty slogan.

We must walk our talk if we are to survive—both individually and collectively. The group must survive, or the individual has no chance to survive. The quality of my sobriety depends upon the quality of your sobriety. We are interconnected through the fellowship of the spirit. We are each responsible for the continued existence of our way of life.

The future of this magnificent cathedral of the spirit is in our hands and rests on the shoulders of those among us who are willing to walk the talk with Step Twelve. We are on the precipice of a turning point for our Twelve Step way of life. It can go either way.

I challenge you to spend as little time as possible talking about the *problem* and spend all of your time carrying the message about the *solution*—ever mindful that carrying the message through Step Twelve is not a message about alcohol or other drugs. It is a message about the healing power of a Power greater than ourselves working in our lives as we live to serve others.

In 1935 a candle was lit. That candle has been passed on to each one of us. Take your light into any dark cave where someone is suffering and pass it on.

What is your Higher Power calling you to do in service?

Acknowledgments

. . . of myself I am nothing. It is my sponsor in the diner who doeth the work.

I wish to express my love and enormous gratitude to the God of my understanding and to my professors at Wilson and Smith University's School of Spiritual Growth: my spiritual advisor Tony A., and my beloved sponsors who helped me get clean and sober and stay that way: Edgar W., Shawn M., Storey T., Chris C., Peter F., Ron McG., Wally P., and especially to Randy F., without whose friendship, support, and guidance this book would not have been written.

I owe a debt of gratitude to my editor Sid Farrar and to Taryn Cross, who contributed prodigious transcription services for this project.

Thanks be to God for crossing my path with so many extraordinary Step Twelve warriors—my true brothers and sisters in the fellowship of the spirit who shared with me their experience, strength, and hope during interviews conducted in preparation for writing this book: Allison H., Amber P., Andrew L., Arisa B., Arnie W., Father Bill, Bob G., Bobby Z., Brave F., Carver B., Columbus, Dan P., Danny F., David A., Gil M., Harry W., James B., Jimmy L., Jody K., John C., John H., John McA., John S., Jordan S., Kameron D., Kerry N., Larry S., LaVerne T., Leonard B., Marie K., Markey F., Mary B., Mel B., Mike F., Mike H., Pat P., Randy F., Richie F., Dr. Rick D., Sheridan O., Suzanne L., Tony A., Troy K., and Wally P.

Forever I will be indebted to Tom P. and Deborah P., who mentored and encouraged me through the process of creating and producing recovery-based entertainment resulting in a Step Twelve ministry and to actors Richard S., John S., and Will S., who portrayed Dr. Bob to my Bill W. as we trudged the road carrying the message of hope through our many national tours of *Pass It On . . . An Evening with Bill W. & Dr. Bob.*

I offer a special heartfelt thank you to the Actors Fund of America for getting me into treatment, and to the world's greatest social worker, Elizabeth Avedon, who helped keep me reasonably sane for decades, patiently listening to my rants and my heart songs and guiding me to find healing from many issues beyond addiction and alcoholism.

Last, but certainly not least, I wish to express my love and gratitude to all of my wonderful pigeons, past and present, who keep me sober one day at a time.

Twelve Step Resources

Alcoholics Anonymous, 4th edition (AA World Services, Inc. 2001)

Twelve Steps and Twelve Traditions (AA World Services, Inc. 2002)

Pass It On: The Story of Bill Wilson and How the AA Message Reached the World (AA World Services, Inc. 1984)

Narcotics Anonymous (NA World Services, 2008)

A Program for You: A Guide to the Big Book's Design for Living (Hazelden Publishing, 1991)

Steps 4–7: A Guide to the Big Book's Design for Living with Yourself, Joanne and James Hubal (Hazelden Publishing, 1991)

Steps 8–12: A Guide to the Big Book's Design for Living with Others, Joanne and James Hubal (Hazelden Publishing, 1991)

Step 12: Carrying the Message, Joseph L. Kellermann (Hazelden Publishing, 1992)

Twelve Step Sponsorship: How It Works, Hamilton B. (Hazelden Publishing, 1996)

The Soul of Sponsorship: The Friendship of Fr. Ed Dowling, S.J. and Bill Wilson in Letters, Robert Fitzgerald, S.J. (Hazelden Publishing, 1995)

The Twelve Steps of Alcoholics Anonymous

1. We admitted we were powerless over alcohol—that our lives had become unmanageable.

2. Came to believe that a Power greater than ourselves could restore us to sanity.

3. Made a decision to turn our will and our lives over to the care of God *as we understood Him.*

4. Made a searching and fearless moral inventory of ourselves.

5. Admitted to God, to ourselves, and to another human being the exact nature of our wrongs.

6. Were entirely ready to have God remove all these defects of character.

7. Humbly asked Him to remove our shortcomings.

8. Made a list of all persons we had harmed, and became willing to make amends to them all.

9. Made direct amends to such people wherever possible, except when to do so would injure them or others.

10. Continued to take personal inventory and when we were wrong promptly admitted it.

11. Sought through prayer and meditation to improve our conscious contact with God *as we understood Him,* praying only for knowledge of His will for us and the power to carry that out.

12. Having had a spiritual awakening as the result of these steps, we tried to carry this message to alcoholics, and to practice these principles in all our affairs.

Alcoholics Anonymous, 4th ed. (New York: Alcoholics Anonymous World Services, 2001), 59–60.

The Twelve Traditions of Alcoholics Anonymous

1. Our common welfare should come first; personal recovery depends upon A.A. unity.

2. For our group purpose there is but one ultimate authority— a loving God as He may express Himself in our group conscience. Our leaders are but trusted servants; they do not govern.

3. The only requirement for A.A. membership is a desire to stop drinking.

4. Each group should be autonomous except in matters affecting other groups or A.A. as a whole.

5. Each group has but one primary purpose—to carry its message to the alcoholic who still suffers.

6. An A.A. group ought never endorse, finance, or lend the A.A. name to any related facility or outside enterprise, lest problems of money, property, and prestige divert us from our primary purpose.

7. Every A.A. group ought to be fully self-supporting, declining outside contributions.

8. Alcoholics Anonymous should remain forever nonprofessional, but our service centers may employ special workers.

9. A.A., as such, ought never be organized; but we may create service boards or committees directly responsible to those they serve.

10. Alcoholics Anonymous has no opinion on outside issues; hence the A.A. name ought never be drawn into public controversy.

11. Our public relations policy is based on attraction rather than promotion; we need always maintain personal anonymity at the level of press, radio, and films.

12. Anonymity is the spiritual foundation of all our traditions, ever reminding us to place principles before personalities.

Twelve Steps and Twelve Traditions (New York: Alcoholics Anonymous World Services, 1981), 129–87.

Bibliography

Alcoholics Anonymous. 2016. "Historical Data: The Birth of A.A. and Its Growth in the U.S./Canada." Accessed August 17, 2016. www.aa.org/pages/en_us/historical-data-the-birth-of-aa-and -its-growth-in-the-uscanada.

Alcoholics Anonymous, 4th Edition. 2001. New York: Alcoholics Anonymous World Services, Inc.

Alcoholics Anonymous Comes of Age: A Brief History of A.A. 1985. New York: Alcoholics Anonymous World Services, Inc.

As Bill Sees It. 1967. New York: Alcoholics Anonymous World Services, Inc.

B., Dick. 2006. "A.A.'s Success Rate Controversies: Do They Matter?" Accessed August 17, 2016. silkworth.net/dickb/success_rate _controversies.html.

Center for Behavioral Health Statistics and Quality. 2015. *Behavioral Health Trends in the United States: results from the 2014 National Survey on Drug Use and Health.* HHS Publication No. SMA 15-4927, NSDUH Series H-50. www.samhsa.gov /data/sites/default/files/NSDUH-FRR1-2014/NSDUH-FRR1 -2014.pdf.

Clark, Walter Houston. 1951. *The Oxford Group–Its History and Significance.* Bookman Associates.

Dr. Bob and the Good Oldtimers. 1980. New York: Alcoholics Anonymous World Services, Inc.

Henry, Bonnie. 1997. "Back to AA's ABCs: Basics Stress God and Short Process." *The Arizona Daily Star.*

A Manual for Alcoholics Anonymous. 1940. Akron, Ohio: Akron Progressive Printing Co.

'Pass It On': The Story of Bill Wilson and How the A.A. Message
Reached the World. 1984. New York: Alcoholics Anonymous
World Services, Inc.

Snyder, Clarence. 1944. *A.A. Sponsorship . . . Its Opportunities and
Its Responsibilities.*

W., Bill. "The Greatest Gift of All." December 1957. *The AA
Grapevine.*

W., Bill. October 1957. *The AA Grapevine.*

W., Bill. November 1960. *The AA Grapevine.*

W., Bill. October 1965. *The AA Grapevine.*

World Health Organization. January 2015. "Alcohol." Last updated
January 2015. www.who.int/mediacentre/factsheets/fs349/en/.

About the Author

Gary K., a grateful recovering alcoholic and addict, travels from coast to coast in the United States and Canada carrying the message of hope and serving as an ambassador for the National Council on Alcoholism and Drug Dependence. He has appeared as a frequent guest on radio and network television advocating for Twelve Step recovery. He is a recovery circuit speaker and Twelve Step historian and educator, facilitating groups in treatment centers and conducting workshops detailing the spiritual principles of the Twelve Steps. He authored, produced, and portrayed the role of Bill W. in five national tours of the live stage production *Pass It On . . . An Evening with Bill W. & Dr. Bob* and has portrayed Bill W. in the travelling production of the Off-Broadway play *Bill W. and Dr. Bob*, which was seen during the 75th International AA Convention. He is also CEO of Unflappable Recovery Entertainment NYC, which is dedicated to celebrating sobriety through the mediums of theater, film, and television, and serves as director of project development for the Recovery Education Campaign Film Project featuring Northern Light Production's documentary *One Day at a Time: The History, Hope, and Healing of 12 Step Recovery,* slated for worldwide broadcast through PBS and the BBC. Learn more about the Recovery Education Campaign Film Project at www.OneDayataTimetheMovie.com. When not on the road, Gary makes his home in Delray Beach, Florida, often referred to as "the recovery capital of the world." You can email Gary K. at PassItOn@Mail2Miracle.com.

About Hazelden Publishing

As part of the Hazelden Betty Ford Foundation, Hazelden Publishing offers both cutting-edge educational resources and inspirational books. Our print and digital works help guide individuals in treatment and recovery, and their loved ones. Professionals who work to prevent and treat addiction also turn to Hazelden Publishing for evidence-based curricula, digital content solutions, and videos for use in schools, treatment programs, correctional programs, and electronic health records systems. We also offer training for implementation of our curricula.

Through published and digital works, Hazelden Publishing extends the reach of healing and hope to individuals, families, and communities affected by addiction and related issues.

For more information about Hazelden publications,
please call **800-328-9000**
or visit us online at **hazelden.org/bookstore**.

Other Titles That May Interest You

Drop the Rock
Removing Character Defects: Steps 6 and 7

Bill P., Todd W., and Sara S.

Based on the principles behind Steps Six and Seven, *Drop the Rock* combines personal stories, practical advice, and powerful insights to help readers move forward in recovery.

Order No. 4291, also available as an e-book

Drop the Rock—The Ripple Effect
Using Step 10 to Work Steps 6 and 7 Every Day

Fred H.

In *Drop the Rock—The Ripple Effect,* Fred H. reveals Step Ten as the natural culmination of working the previous Steps.

Order No. 9743, also available as an e-book

12 Hidden Rewards of Making Amends
Finding Forgiveness and Self-Respect by Working Steps 8–10

Allen Berger, PhD

Popular author and lecturer Allen Berger, PhD, shares more profound recovery insight in *12 Hidden Rewards of Making Amends* and motivates us to earn the rewards that come with being honest and vulnerable.

Order No. 3968, also available as an e-book

Hazelden Publishing books are available at fine bookstores everywhere. To order from Hazelden Publishing, call **800-328-9000** or visit **hazelden.org/bookstore**.